FROM NOISE TO SIGNAL

KATHRYN OTTE SCOTT

ISBN: 979-8-89901-537-3

ISBN: 979-8-218-67546-2

Published by:

Kathryn Scott
on behalf of THE COLLECTIVE STORY LAB,
an imprint of THE COLLECTIVE LLC (www.thecollectiveagency.cc)

Printed in the United States of America
First Edition

Kathryn Otte Scott is a publishing name used by Kathryn Scott.

FROM NOISE TO SIGNAL

To Devlin - your story matters.

To Iain & Aldin - keep writing your story.

CONTENTS

INTRODUCTION

OH HEY!

Welcome to *From Noise to Signal: Creating high-impact content that captures your customer's attention.*

Today, information overload is the norm and attention spans are suffering, standing out amidst the noise has become more challenging than ever. As a communicator with two decades of experience, I understand the frustration and uncertainty that many businesses face when trying to capture the attention of their target audience.

In this book, we'll take a journey together to demystify the art and science of creating content that not only cuts through the clutter but also resonates deeply with your audience. Whether you're a seasoned communicator or marketer looking to refine your strategies or a small business owner seeking to make a big impact on a limited budget, this guide is designed to provide you with practical insights and actionable tips to elevate your content game.

Throughout these pages, we'll delve into the nuances of understanding your audience, crafting compelling messages, choosing the right channels, and creating attention-grabbing content that leaves a lasting impression. But more than just theory, we'll explore real-world examples and emerging trends to inspire and empower you to take your content to new heights.

Above all, this book is a testament to the power of communication in fostering meaningful connections with your audience. It's about more than just selling products or services—it's about building trust, establishing credibility, and ultimately, creating a community of loyal advocates for your brand.

So, I invite you to join me as we transform noise into signal and make a lasting impact in the hearts and minds of your customers.

1

KNOW THY AUDIENCE

FROM NOISE TO SIGNAL

CHAPTER I. KNOW THY AUDIENCE

THE FIRST STEP TO MAKING EVERY MESSAGE COUNT

DIVE INTO THE DEEP END

In the dynamics of business, understanding your audience isn't just a strategy—it's a journey of empathy and insight. Take the time to immerse yourself in the world of your customers so that you can concretely understand their needs, desires, and pain points. Through market research, surveys, and genuine conversations, you can uncover the nuances of their preferences and behaviors. Remember, your audience isn't just a demographic—they're real people with unique stories. By delving into their world with curiosity, you can gain invaluable insights that shape your content strategy and create genuine connections.

PINPOINT THE PAIN POINTS AND DESIRES

Identifying customer pain points and desires is the cornerstone of effective communication for small business owners. Take a strategic approach to understanding what keeps your customers up at night and what drives them to seek solutions like yours. This involves not only listening to their feedback but also observing their behaviors and analyzing trends in the market. By pinpointing these pain points and desires, you can tailor your messaging and content to resonate with your audience to meet them where they are, offering solutions that address their needs and their aspirations without them even telling you directly.

HUMANIZE YOUR AUDIENCE

Crafting detailed buyer personas, or profiles, is essential for small business owners seeking to connect with their target audience in meaningful ways. These personas go beyond demographics - they must paint a vivid picture of the individuals who interact with your brand. To do this, you need to identify key characteristics, motivations, and, yes, pain points that define your ideal customers.

PERSONAS FOR ALEX'S FRUIT STAND

BUYER PERSONA 1: HARPER

Age: 40
Gender: Non-binary
Occupation: Wellness Coach
Income Level: Middle to Upper Class
Location: Urban/Suburban Area

INTERESTS AND BEHAVIORS:

- Values health and wellness
- Prefers organic and locally-sourced produce
- Regularly practices yoga and meditation
- Active on social media, especially Instagram, for fitness and healthy lifestyle inspiration
- Enjoys trying new recipes and experimenting with fresh ingredients

BUYING MOTIVATIONS:

1. Seeks nutritious and high-quality fruits for smoothies, salads, and snacks
2. Supports local businesses and sustainable farming practices
3. Values convenience and accessibility of fresh produce

BUYER PERSONA 2: JACK

Age: 30
Gender: Male
Occupation: Freelance Graphic Designer
Income Level: Middle Class
Location: Urban Area

INTERESTS AND BEHAVIORS:

- Leads a fast-paced lifestyle with demanding work hours
- Often eats on-the-go or orders takeout
- Tries to maintain a healthy diet but lacks time for meal preparation
- Tech-savvy and relies on mobile apps for convenience
- Values efficiency and convenience in shopping experiences

BUYING MOTIVATIONS:

1. Seeks quick and convenient options
2. Prefers pre-cut and pre-packaged fruit options for easy consumption
3. Values speed and efficiency in purchasing process

BUYER PERSONA 3: BAILEY

Age: 50
Gender: Female
Occupation: Social Worker
Income Level: Lower to Middle Class
Location: Suburban/Rural Area

INTERESTS AND BEHAVIORS:

- Manages a household on a tight budget
- Prioritizes saving money on groceries and household expenses
- Enjoys cooking and baking for her family
- Values community and local businesses
- Shops at farmers' markets and seeks deals and discounts

BUYING MOTIVATIONS:

1. Seeks affordable and fresh fruit options for her family's meals and snacks
2. Values the quality and flavor of locally-grown produce at reasonable prices
3. Prefers bulk purchasing options and seasonal discounts

Buyer personas help you humanize your audience, which allows you to tailor your content and message where you speak to and from their point of view. Remember, each persona represents a unique opportunity to build trust and foster loyalty with your audience, so invest the time and effort to create personas that truly resonate with your brand.

KNOW THY COMPETITORS

To truly connect with your audience, you must first understand who else is competing for their attention. Knowing your competitors is just as important as knowing your audience. You can't craft compelling messages or choose the right channels if you're unaware of who else is speaking to your audience, and how they're doing it. Competitors can offer valuable insights into the preferences, behaviors, and expectations of your shared audience. By studying their strengths and weaknesses, you can identify gaps in the market and capitalize on opportunities that others might have missed.

Understanding your competitors also helps you differentiate your brand. It allows you to spot trends, leverage unique value propositions, and tailor your messaging in a way that resonates more deeply with your audience. In a crowded digital space, knowing both your audience and your competitors is the key to standing out and creating meaningful connections.

BRAND POSITIONING

DESCRIBING YOUR AUDIENCE

AGE RANGE OF YOUR TARGET AUDIENCE

DO THEY HAVE CHILDREN?

IS THERE A PRIMARY GENDER CATEGORY?

WHERE DO THEY LIVE?

WHAT IS THE HIGHEST LEVEL OF EDUCATION?

WHAT JOBS DO THEY HAVE?

WHAT IS THEIR MARITAL STATUS?

WHAT IS THEIR INCOME LEVEL?

WHAT ARE THEIR FEARS AND CONCERNS?

SELECT THE 3 MOST IMPORTANT ASPECTS TO YOUR CUSTOMER:

PRICE	SPEED	FLEXIBILITY
QUALITY	SERVICE	DEPENDABILITY

WHAT ARE THE CAUSES THEY SUPPORT?

WHAT ARE THEIR HOBBIES?

BRAND POSITIONING

AUDIENCE AND COMPETITORS

DOES YOUR TARGET AUDIENCE CURRENTLY BUY SOMETHING LIKE YOU'RE SELLING?

HOW IS YOUR PRODUCT SOLVING THEIR PROBLEM?

WHAT WOULD HOLD THEM BACK FROM BUYING YOUR PRODUCT OR SERVICE?

WHAT PUSHES THEM TO MAKE PURCHASING DECISIONS?

WHO IS YOUR COMPETITION?

WHAT DIFFERENTIATES YOU FROM YOUR COMPETITION?

HOW INFORMED ARE CUSTOMERS ABOUT YOUR TOPIC, INDUSTRY, OR COMPANY?

DOES YOUR BUSINESS IDEA NEED TO BE ALTERED TO BETTER APPEAL TO THIS AUDIENCE?

HOW CAN YOU BEST REACH THEM (ADVERTISING, WEBSITE, SOCIAL MEDIA ETC.)?

BRAND POSITIONING

COMPETITOR ANALYSIS

Identify the strengths and weaknesses of your rivals. Analyze their marketing, pricing, promotion channels, market share, and other details

	COMPETITOR 1	COMPETITOR 2	COMPETITOR 3
SUMMARY Describe what you already know about them			
STRENGTHS			
WEAKNESSES			
TARGET AUDIENCE			
PRODUCT OR SERVICE PRICING			
GENERAL MARKETING STRATEGY			
ONLINE MARKETING STRATEGY			
COMPETITIVE ADVANTAGE			
THREATS			
OPPORTUNITIES			

BRAND POSITIONING

PRODUCT/SERVICE ANALYSIS

Assess how your product/service/team compares to competitors.

ASSESSMENT	WE/COMP.	NAME OF SKILLS	IMPORTANCE TO CUSTOMER					
			1	2	3	4	5	6
UNIQUE SKILLS	WE							
	COMPETITOR							
BEST SKILLS	WE							
	COMPETITOR							
SAME SKILLS	WE							
	COMPETITOR							
LOW SKILLS	WE							
	COMPETITOR							

2

MESSAGES THAT MATTER

FROM NOISE TO SIGNAL

CHAPTER II. MESSAGES THAT MATTER

GRAB ATTENTION AND DRIVE ACTION

DEFINING YOUR BRAND VOICE AND TONE

Crafting a distinct brand voice and tone is a fundamental pillar of successful communication, particularly for small business owners who are trying to carve out their own niche in a crowded marketplace. Your brand's voice is its unique personality—it's how you present yourself to the world, how you speak to your customers, and the essence of what you stand for. Your tone, on the other hand, refers to the emotional inflections you apply to your communication. It's the mood you set, whether lighthearted, serious, passionate, or authoritative, that colors how your audience perceives your messages.

To define your brand voice and tone, it's important to start by reflecting on the heart of your business—your core values, your mission, and the audience you're aiming to connect with. Are you targeting a more professional, no-nonsense crowd that appreciates clarity and authority, or are you speaking to a younger, trend-conscious demographic that values a fun, conversational approach? To help you nail this down, refer back to the buyer personas you've created, as they provide a deep dive into the behaviors, preferences, and pain points of your target market.

Once you have a clear picture of your audience, think about the emotions you want to evoke with your messaging. Do you want your audience to feel inspired, reassured, or excited? How do you want them to feel after interacting with your brand—empowered, informed, or entertained? Consider how your communication style aligns with your overall brand identity and ensure that it reflects the core mission of your business.

Above all, consistency is key. Your brand voice and tone should be cohesive across all of your touchpoints, from your website and social media to customer service interactions and marketing materials. This consistency helps build trust and familiarity, making your audience feel like they know who you are and what you stand for. Remember, the way you speak to your audience is often what hooks them in and keeps them coming back for more.

It can also be helpful to look at other content that resonates with you. Think about the types of publications, blogs, or brands you engage with regularly—what's their tone and voice? Why do you gravitate toward their content over others? By analyzing what works for you as a consumer, you can glean valuable insights into how to develop your own brand voice and tone that resonates just as strongly with your audience.

DEFINING YOUR BRAND WORDS & CHARACTER

The words you use to express your brand are like the clothes it wears. They're the outward expression of your brand's personality, the language that connects you to your audience, and what sets you apart from everyone else. These brand words aren't just about filling space—they're about packing meaning into every sentence, phrase, and tagline.

When you pick your brand words, you're choosing how your brand speaks to the world. Whether it's the tone in a post or the tagline on a billboard, every word you use communicates something important about who you are. Brand words help reinforce your values, show your personality, and create a lasting impression in your audience's minds. So, it's important to think about what kind of feeling you want to evoke.

You can also think about the emotional side of your words. Are you trying to inspire confidence, make someone laugh, or make your audience feel like they belong? Choose words that elicit those feelings. Your choice of words directly influences how your audience perceives your brand and helps you create that connection that makes people want to engage with your business.

Brand words also speak to the personality behind your brand—this is your brand character. Just like a person has a personality, your brand has one too, and it's shaped by the words you use. Think of it this way: Your brand's character should match the tone of voice you want to project, whether that's down-to-earth, fun, professional, or inspiring. If your brand were a person, how would they act in a conversation? Would they be playful and casual, or more serious and knowledgeable?

Once you've nailed down your brand's character and the words that reflect it, consistency is key. You want these words to pop up in all your marketing materials, social media posts, emails—basically everywhere. The more your audience hears and reads these words, the more they start to associate them with your brand.

As you refine your brand's identity, keep an eye on how your brand words and character evolve. Just like people grow and change, your brand can too. You might find that as your business expands or your audience changes, your words might need a little refresh to keep up. But make sure the core of your brand character stays consistent so you don't lose the essence of who you are.

In the end, your brand words and character aren't just about sounding good—they're about creating a genuine connection with your audience. They help you tell your story in a way that's memorable and meaningful, so your customers feel like they really "get" you. When you take the time to choose your words thoughtfully and build a solid brand character, you'll be setting yourself up for success that goes beyond just what you sell—it's about how you make people feel when they interact with your brand.

DEVELOPING A UNIQUE SELLING PROPOSITION

Standing out is a non-negotiable necessity. That's where a Unique Selling Proposition (USP) comes in. Your USP is the defining statement that encapsulates what makes your brand unique—why should customers choose you over all the other options out there? It's the special ingredient that sets you apart and adds real value to your customers' lives.

To craft your USP, begin by reflecting on your strengths and the qualities that distinguish you from your competitors. Do you offer exceptional quality, unmatched customer service, or innovative solutions? Whether it's a product feature that no one else offers, a level of personalized service that competitors can't match, or your dedication to sustainability, pinpoint what makes your business stand out. Once you've identified these key differentiators, distill them into a clear and concise proposition that speaks directly to the needs and desires of your target audience.

Your USP should not only be clear but also memorable. It should be a phrase or statement that sticks with your customers, creating a strong association between your brand and the value you provide. When you communicate your USP effectively, you are positioning yourself as the obvious choice in the minds of consumers, ultimately making it easier to attract new customers while retaining loyal ones who recognize the unique benefits you offer.

But don't just stop there—be sure to weave your USP into your messaging and communication across all platforms. From your website copy to your social media posts, your USP should be a thread that runs through everything you do. When executed properly, your USP not only sets you apart from competitors but also builds a deeper emotional connection with your audience, fostering long-term relationships and loyalty.

STORYTELLING TECHNIQUES

Everyone loves a good story. It's why we binge-watch great television shows and what keeps us turning the pages of a book series. Stories bring brands to life. Harnessing the power of storytelling is a cornerstone of effective communication, period. Stories have a unique ability to captivate audiences, evoke emotions, and convey messages in a memorable way.

Consider the narrative arc (I know, fancy term!) of your brand—what challenges have you overcome, what successes have you achieved, what impact has your business had on your customers, and why did you start your business in the first place? Authenticity is key—sharing genuine stories that resonate with your audience deepens trust with your customers and helps them relate to you and the products and services you offer.

One of the most effective ways to incorporate storytelling into your business communication is by using various forms of content. Blog posts, social media updates, customer testimonials, and case studies all offer great opportunities to tell stories that resonate with your audience. These narratives not only provide valuable insights into your brand but also allow your audience to see themselves in your story.

In the end, great storytelling should inspire action. Whether it's a customer choosing to purchase your product, sign up for your newsletter, or share your content with their network, your stories should drive real engagement and foster a sense of loyalty among your audience. The goal is to make your customers walk away saying, "Yes! They get it!" When you can tap into the power of storytelling and craft compelling narratives, you build a strong emotional connection that keeps customers coming back for more.

BRAND MESSAGING

FINDING YOUR BRAND WORDS

ACTIVE	CRAFTY	INSPIRATIONAL	SERIOUS
ADVENTUROUS	CULTURED	INTENTIONAL	SINCERE
AMBITIOUS	DARING	INVITING	SOPHISTICATED
APPROACHABLE	DELICATE	JOYFUL	TIMELESS
BOHEMIAN	DOWN TO EARTH	KIND	TRADITIONAL
BOLD	DYNAMIC	LIVELY	TRANSPARENT
BRAVE	EDGY	LOYAL	TRENDY
BRIGHT	ELEGANT	LUXURIOUS	TRUSTWORTHY
BUBBLY	FEARLESS	MAGICAL	UPLIFTING
CALM	FUN	MATURE	URBAN
CANDID	GENUINE	MINIMAL	WARM
CAREFREE	HARMONIOUS	MODERN	WHIMSICAL
CASUAL	HEARTFELT	NATURAL	WILD
CHARMING	HELPFUL	PLAYFUL	WISDOM
CHEERFUL	HIGH-END	POSITIVE	WITTY
CLASSIC	HONEST	PROFESSIONAL	WONDERFUL
COLLABORATIVE	HOPEFUL	QUIRKY	YOUTHFUL
COLORFUL	INCLUSIVE	RELAXED	ZANY
COOL	INDUSTRIAL	ROMANTIC	ZEALOUS
COZY	INNOVATIVE	SASSY	

NARROW THEM DOWN TO THE 5 BEST FITTING WORDS

BRAND MESSAGING

WHAT IS YOUR BRAND VOICE?

Find three words that best represent your brand and complete the chart

BECAUSE WE VALUE	OUR VOICE IS	THIS MEANS OUR COMMUNICATION IS	BUT NOT
FOR EXAMPLE: ORIGINALITY	CONFIDENT	BOLD CREATIVE VISIONARY	ARROGANT STANDARDLESS BLUNT

Think about the words that describe your business. Then carefully pick the adjectives, nouns, verbs and other parts of speech that you want to relate to your business and also those you would like to avoid.

WHY DO I NEED THIS?

GOOD BRAND VOICE MAKES YOUR BRAND STAND OUT FROM THE NOISE, AND HELPS CONSUMERS REMEMBER AND RELATE TO YOUR BRAND. THIS, IN TURN, CREATES STRONGER BRAND LOYALITY.

UNDERSTANDING YOUR UNIQUE SELLING POINT

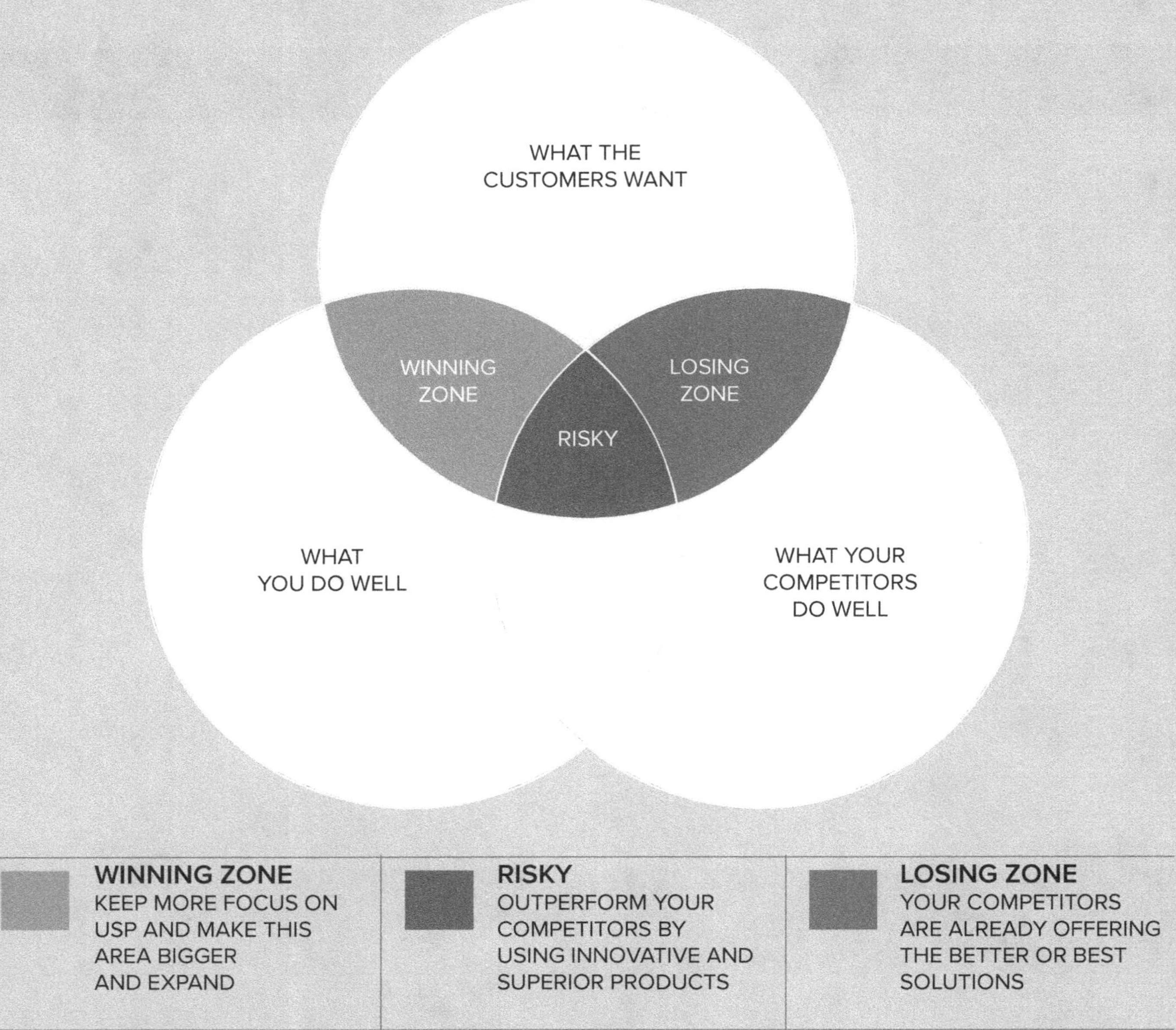

WINNING ZONE	RISKY	LOSING ZONE
KEEP MORE FOCUS ON USP AND MAKE THIS AREA BIGGER AND EXPAND	OUTPERFORM YOUR COMPETITORS BY USING INNOVATIVE AND SUPERIOR PRODUCTS	YOUR COMPETITORS ARE ALREADY OFFERING THE BETTER OR BEST SOLUTIONS

A unique selling proposition is a short sentence highlighting the competitive advantage that makes your business stand out from its competitors. It should help people quickly understand why they should choose you over another company.

CONTENT IDEAS

SOCIAL MEDIA

SHARE A PORTFOLIO ITEM	SHARE BEHIND THE SCENES	SHARE A HELPFUL TIP IN YOUR NICHE	SHARE A STORY OF YOUR STRUGGLE	SHARE A CUSTOMER PHOTO OF YOUR PRODUCT
SHARE WHAT INSPIRES YOU	SHARE A CLIENT TESTIMONIAL	SHARE A POSITIVE AFFIRMATION	DO AN "ASK ME ANYHING" SESSION	SHARE A STORY OF HOW YOU GOT STARTED

LEAD MAGNETS

PDF GUIDE	EBOOK	USEFUL WORKSHEET	DISCOUNT CODE	ASSESMENT TEST
PLANNER	PDF LIST (EX. "50 BEST EMAIL HEADLINES")	USEFUL RESOUCE LIST	QUIZ / SURVEY	FREE TRIAL

BLOG CONTENT

WRITE ABOUT YOUR PROCESS	CREATE A TUTORIAL	USE QUORA QUESTIONS AS INSPIRATION FOR BLOG POST IDEAS	WRITE "TOP 10" STYLE BLOG POSTS	WRITE ABOUT MUST HAVE SKILLS IN YOUR NICHE
SHARE YOUR INSIGHTS	DO A COMPARISON POST	LIST HACKS & TIME SAVERS	WRITE A HELPFUL REVIEW	USE YOUTUBE VIDEOS FOR INSPIRATIONS FOR YOUR BLOG POSTS

3

WHERE TO PLAY

CHAPTER III. WHERE TO PLAY

MAKE YOUR VOICE HEARD WHERE IT MATTERS MOST

NAVIGATING CONTENT DISTRIBUTION CHANNELS FOR SUCCESS

Navigating the multitude of content distribution channels can be overwhelming for small business owners, but understanding the options available is crucial for reaching your target audience effectively. From social media platforms like Facebook, Instagram, LinkedIn, and X to email marketing, blogs, and video-sharing sites, each channel offers unique opportunities for engagement and exposure.

Consider the demographics, preferences, and behaviors of your audience to determine which channels are most relevant to your brand. Remember, quality over quantity—focusing on a few key channels where your audience is most active allows you to allocate resources efficiently and maximize your impact.

Here's how I define the leading external channels to help me decide which channels to spend my time and energy:

- Facebook is my inner circle community and family
- Instagram is my friends, and it's about showing, not telling
- LinkedIn is for my colleagues
- X, Threads, Bluesky is for acquaintances where I can give and receive quick updates, breaking news, and rant or debate
- Video-sharing sites like YouTube or Reels on Instagram and TikTok are for scrollers who might be strangers but are looking to be entertained or inspired

I know you were studious enough to work on your buyer personas in the last chapter, so you'll be able to determine which channel your ideal personas fit in. Once you determine that, stick to the ones that have the biggest impact, and cut out the rest. Less is more when it comes to content impact where there are so many different places it can live.

SELECTING CHANNELS BASED ON AUDIENCE DEMOGRAPHICS AND PREFERENCES

When it comes to selecting content distribution channels, small business owners must prioritize relevance and resonance with their target audience. Take the time to analyze the demographics and preferences of your audience to identify which channels align best with their needs and interests.

For example, if your target demographic consists primarily of professionals, platforms like LinkedIn or Instagram may be more effective than traditional email marketing or Facebook. By tailoring your channel selection to the characteristics of your audience, you can ensure that your content reaches the right people in the right places, increasing the likelihood of engagement and conversion.

If you're targeting older generations or a more family-oriented audience, platforms like Facebook or email might be more effective. Older consumers often appreciate detailed content, personalized customer service, and straightforward messaging, which are strengths of these channels.

On the other hand, younger, trend-driven consumers might be more inclined to engage with brands through platforms like TikTok, Instagram, or X, where they can interact with bite-sized content, dynamic visuals, and influencer-led campaigns. Understanding these nuances and aligning your strategies accordingly can help you reach your audience where they are most likely to engage.

STRATEGIES FOR MAXIMIZING REACH AND IMPACT ON CHOSEN CHANNELS

Once you've identified the most suitable content distribution channels for your brand, it's essential to develop strategies for maximizing your reach and impact. This involves creating compelling content tailored to each channel's format and audience preferences, as well as optimizing your timing and frequency of posting to maximize visibility.

Each platform has its own unique set of best practices. For example, Instagram thrives on visual storytelling—high-quality images, videos, and Reels are the stars of the show. Meanwhile, X/Threads/Bluesky are built for brevity, where sharp, witty statements, quick updates, and engaging with trending topics are essential for success. LinkedIn, on the other hand, is a more professional space, where long-form content, thought leadership posts, and industry insights tend to resonate. By understanding what works on each platform, you can tailor your content strategy to engage users in ways that feel native to the environment they're browsing.

Beyond content creation, timing plays a significant role in your strategy. Posting when your audience is most active increases your chances of visibility. For example, early mornings and late afternoons might be prime times for engaging busy professionals on LinkedIn, while evenings and weekends could be better for family-oriented or entertainment-based content on Facebook. Be sure to track your engagement metrics and adjust your timing based on the behavior of your specific audience.

Additionally, engaging with your audience through comments, messages, and shares fosters a sense of community and loyalty around your brand. Responding to customer inquiries, starting conversations, and sharing user-generated content can help deepen relationships and build brand advocates who will organically spread the word about your business.

Another powerful tool for maximizing impact is utilizing content repurposing. Instead of creating entirely new content for each channel, find ways to recycle and adapt content for different formats. A long-form blog post could be condensed into an engaging Instagram carousel, or a webinar can be broken down into bite-sized clips. This not only saves time but ensures your content gets the exposure it deserves across various platforms.

Finally, don't forget to measure and analyze your results regularly. Use platform analytics and audience insights to gauge what's working and what's not. Refining your strategies based on performance data is key to continuously improving your approach. By staying flexible and adaptable, you can fine-tune your content distribution to achieve the highest possible engagement and return on investment.

On the next page, you'll see an easy-to-follow chart with a rubric of questions, potential conclusions, and example channels. This will help guide you through the process of evaluating your chosen channels and refining your content distribution strategy for maximum success.

PLANNING CAMPAIGNS AND APPROPRIATELY LEVERAGING A MULTI-CHANNEL APPROACH

Planning effective campaigns is essential for driving engagement, building brand awareness, and ultimately increasing conversions. While focusing on a single channel might feel like the most straightforward approach, leveraging multiple channels strategically allows you to meet your audience where they are and amplify your message across various touchpoints. A multi-channel approach maximizes reach, enhances your brand presence, and ensures that your campaign resonates with diverse segments of your audience.

To get started with planning a campaign, first, define your goals clearly. What do you want to achieve with this campaign? Whether it's increasing website traffic, driving sales, promoting a new product, or raising awareness about an event, your goals should guide your campaign's structure, messaging, and the channels you choose to use. Without a clear objective, it's easy to get distracted and lose focus on delivering impactful results.

1. UNDERSTAND YOUR AUDIENCE AND CHANNEL ALIGNMENT

The success of your campaign depends heavily on selecting the right channels. Take into account the nuances of your audience's preferences and behaviors across different platforms. For example, you might want to use Instagram for visual storytelling and Facebook for deeper engagement with your community. If you're promoting an industry event, LinkedIn might be the right place to engage with professionals, while platforms like X could be ideal for real-time updates or to spark conversations about trending topics.

A multi-channel approach allows you to meet your audience wherever they are, but it's important that each channel's role is well defined. For instance, use email marketing to send personalized offers or detailed updates, while social media platforms can help generate buzz and conversation. With a clear understanding of what each channel brings to the table, you can create a campaign that uses each platform to its full potential.

2. CRAFT CONSISTENT, TAILORED MESSAGING ACROSS CHANNELS

Once you've mapped out which channels you'll be using, focus on crafting messaging that resonates with your audience, yet is tailored to each channel's format. It's important to keep the overall messaging consistent, but adapt the tone and style to match the medium. For example, on Instagram, visual content like images or Reels should be the star, accompanied by short, impactful captions. For LinkedIn, you might lean into more professional language and longer posts that share insights or thought leadership.

Even with a multi-channel strategy, keep your messaging coherent to reinforce your brand identity. A well-coordinated campaign across multiple platforms creates a seamless experience for your audience, allowing them to feel like they're interacting with the same brand across each touchpoint, rather than feeling like they are engaging with separate entities.

3. OPTIMIZE TIMING AND FREQUENCY FOR EACH CHANNEL

One of the key benefits of a multi-channel approach is the ability to optimize your campaign's reach by scheduling posts at times when your audience is most active on each platform. While Facebook and LinkedIn may see the most engagement during weekday mornings or late afternoons, Instagram and X often see higher activity in the evenings or on weekends.

Consider the frequency of posts as well. On Instagram, you might post daily or every other day, but for email campaigns, it may make sense to send more occasional, higher-value messages that drive action. By tailoring the timing and frequency for each channel, you ensure your content isn't overwhelming your audience but still remains top of mind.

4. USE CROSS-PROMOTION TO STRENGTHEN THE CAMPAIGN

To create synergy between your channels, consider cross-promotion. For example, promote your Instagram contest or campaign on your Facebook page, or share snippets from a recent YouTube video on your feed. This allows you to guide your audience through multiple channels while maintaining the same core messaging, increasing the chances they'll engage with your campaign in various ways.

If you're running a giveaway, direct people from Instagram to enter via your website, and then email the winners, creating a seamless flow across channels. Not only does this keep the campaign fresh, but it also helps you extend the lifecycle of your content, ensuring it reaches different audience segments at different times and through different formats.

5. MEASURE, ANALYZE, AND REFINE

A multi-channel approach requires ongoing monitoring and analysis. Use the analytics tools provided by each platform to track how your campaign is performing across different channels. Are people engaging more on Instagram than on LinkedIn? Are email open rates as high as you hoped? What time of day is yielding the most interaction?

By constantly measuring your results, you can refine your strategy in real-time. If a specific platform isn't working as well as expected, consider adjusting the content or shifting resources to a more effective channel. Understanding which channels deliver the best ROI allows you to fine-tune your approach and focus your efforts where it matters most.

BRINGING IT ALL TOGETHER: THE POWER OF A UNIFIED MULTI-CHANNEL CAMPAIGN

Planning and executing a multi-channel campaign can be a game changer for small business owners. It ensures your message reaches your audience at various touchpoints and in formats that best suit their preferences. However, it's essential to approach this strategy with careful planning, smart timing, and consistent messaging.

A successful multi-channel campaign requires integration across channels—each one should work in harmony to tell the same story, making sure your audience has the best chance to connect with your brand. When done right, this approach not only broadens your reach but helps build stronger, more meaningful connections with your audience, increasing your chances for success and growth.

CHANNEL RUBRIC

CRITERIA	QUESTIONS TO ASK YOURSELF	POTENTIAL CONCLUSIONS	EXAMPLE CHANNELS
TARGET AUDIENCE	1. WHO IS MY TARGET AUDIENCE?	IDENTIFY THE CHANNELS WHERE YOUR TARGET AUDIENCE IS MOST ACTIVE.	FACEBOOK, INSTAGRAM, LINKEDIN, TIKTOK, X, YOUTUBE
	2. WHERE DOES MY TARGET AUDIENCE SPEND THEIR TIME ONLINE/OFFLINE?	FOCUS ON CHANNELS FREQUENTED BY YOUR TARGET AUDIENCE (E.G., SOCIAL MEDIA PLATFORMS, INDUSTRY-SPECIFIC FORUMS).	PINTEREST (DIY, CRAFTS), REDDIT (SPECIFIC INTEREST COMMUNITIES), INDUSTRY-SPECIFIC FORUMS OR BLOGS
	3. WHAT ARE THE DEMOGRAPHICS (AGE, GENDER, LOCATION, INTERESTS) OF MY TARGET AUDIENCE?	CHOOSE CHANNELS THAT ALIGN WITH THE DEMOGRAPHICS OF YOUR TARGET AUDIENCE (E.G., INSTAGRAM FOR YOUNGER DEMOGRAPHICS).	SNAPCHAT (YOUNGER AUDIENCE), PINTEREST (FEMALE DEMOGRAPHIC), LINKEDIN (PROFESSIONAL AUDIENCE)
BUDGET	1. WHAT IS MY MARKETING BUDGET?	ALLOCATE BUDGET TO CHANNELS THAT OFFER THE BEST ROI AND ALIGN WITH YOUR OVERALL MARKETING STRATEGY.	GOOGLE ADS, FACEBOOK ADS, INSTAGRAM ADS, LINKEDIN ADS, INFLUENCER PARTNERSHIPS
	2. HOW MUCH AM I WILLING TO ALLOCATE TO EACH MARKETING CHANNEL?	PRIORITIZE CHANNELS THAT CAN DELIVER RESULTS WITHIN YOUR BUDGET CONSTRAINTS.	CONTENT MARKETING (BLOGGING, SEO), EMAIL MARKETING, SOCIAL MEDIA MANAGEMENT TOOLS
GOALS	1. WHAT ARE MY MARKETING GOALS (E.G., BRAND AWARENESS, LEAD GENERATION, SALES CONVERSION)?	SELECT CHANNELS THAT ARE BEST SUITED TO ACHIEVE YOUR SPECIFIC MARKETING GOALS.	BRAND AWARENESS: PR CAMPAIGNS, SOCIAL MEDIA ENGAGEMENT; LEAD GENERATION: GATED CONTENT, EMAIL SIGN-UPS; SALES CONVERSION: RETARGETING ADS, PERSONALIZED EMAILS
	2. WHICH MARKETING CHANNELS ALIGN BEST WITH MY GOALS?	FOCUS ON CHANNELS THAT HAVE A TRACK RECORD OF SUCCESS IN MEETING SIMILAR OBJECTIVES.	BRAND AWARENESS: SOCIAL MEDIA ADS, INFLUENCER MARKETING; LEAD GENERATION: CONTENT MARKETING, PPC ADS; SALES CONVERSION: EMAIL MARKETING, REMARKETING ADS

CHANNEL RUBRIC

CRITERIA	QUESTIONS TO ASK YOURSELF	POTENTIAL CONCLUSIONS	EXAMPLE CHANNELS
GOALS, CONT.	3. HOW WILL I MEASURE THE SUCCESS OF EACH MARKETING CHANNEL IN ACHIEVING MY GOALS?	CHOOSE CHANNELS THAT ALLOW FOR CLEAR MEASUREMENT OF KEY PERFORMANCE INDICATORS RELATED TO YOUR GOALS.	BRAND AWARENESS: IMPRESSIONS, REACH, ENGAGEMENT RATE; LEAD GENERATION: CONVERSION RATE, LEAD QUALITY; SALES CONVERSION: ROI, CONVERSION RATE
BRAND IMAGE	1. WHAT IMAGE OR PERCEPTION DO I WANT MY BRAND TO CONVEY?	OPT FOR CHANNELS THAT ENABLE YOU TO REINFORCE THE DESIRED BRAND IMAGE EFFECTIVELY.	VISUAL PLATFORMS LIKE INSTAGRAM, PINTEREST FOR LIFESTYLE BRANDS; PROFESSIONAL PLATFORMS LIKE LINKEDIN FOR CORPORATE BRANDS; QUIRKY PLATFORMS LIKE TIKTOK FOR YOUTHFUL BRANDS
	2. WHICH MARKETING CHANNELS CAN HELP ME REINFORCE THIS BRAND IMAGE EFFECTIVELY?	SELECT CHANNELS THAT RESONATE WITH THE TONE, VALUES, AND PERSONALITY OF YOUR BRAND.	HUMOROUS BRAND: SOCIAL MEDIA PLATFORMS FOR WITTY CONTENT; LUXURY BRAND: HIGH-QUALITY IMAGERY ON INSTAGRAM, LINKEDIN; ECO-FRIENDLY BRAND: SUSTAINABILITY-FOCUSED CONTENT ON BLOGS, SOCIAL MEDIA
INDUSTRY	1. WHAT MARKETING CHANNELS ARE COMMONLY USED BY BUSINESSES IN MY INDUSTRY?	CONSIDER INDUSTRY NORMS BUT ALSO EXPLORE CHANNELS THAT OFFER OPPORTUNITIES FOR DIFFERENTIATION.	E-COMMERCE: GOOGLE SHOPPING, AMAZON ADS; REAL ESTATE: ZILLOW, REAL ESTATE LISTING WEBSITES; HOSPITALITY: TRIPADVISOR, YELP
	2. ARE THERE ANY INDUSTRY-SPECIFIC REGULATIONS OR RESTRICTIONS THAT AFFECT MY CHOICE OF MARKETING CHANNELS?	ENSURE COMPLIANCE WITH REGULATIONS WHILE EXPLORING CHANNELS THAT OFFER THE BEST POTENTIAL FOR GROWTH.	HEALTH INDUSTRY: HIPAA COMPLIANCE FOR EMAIL MARKETING, FDA REGULATIONS FOR ADVERTISING; FINANCIAL INDUSTRY: SEC REGULATIONS FOR ADVERTISING, DATA PROTECTION LAWS

CHANNEL RUBRIC

CRITERIA	QUESTIONS TO ASK YOURSELF	POTENTIAL CONCLUSIONS	EXAMPLE CHANNELS
TIME & RESOURCES	1. HOW MUCH TIME DO I HAVE AVAILABLE TO DEDICATE TO MARKETING ACTIVITIES?	PRIORITIZE CHANNELS THAT CAN BE EFFECTIVELY MANAGED WITHIN YOUR AVAILABLE TIME AND RESOURCES.	SOCIAL MEDIA MANAGEMENT TOOLS FOR SCHEDULING AND AUTOMATION, OUTSOURCING CONTENT CREATION, EMAIL MARKETING AUTOMATION TOOLS
	2. DO I HAVE THE NECESSARY RESOURCES (PERSONNEL, TOOLS, EXPERTISE) TO MANAGE EACH MARKETING CHANNEL EFFECTIVELY?	CHOOSE CHANNELS THAT MATCH YOUR AVAILABLE RESOURCES AND EXPERTISE TO MAXIMIZE EFFICIENCY AND EFFECTIVENESS.	VIDEO PRODUCTION CAPABILITIES FOR YOUTUBE, GRAPHIC DESIGN SKILLS FOR VISUAL PLATFORMS LIKE INSTAGRAM, EMAIL MARKETING EXPERTISE FOR EMAIL CAMPAIGNS
COMPETITION	1. WHO ARE MY MAIN COMPETITORS AND WHAT MARKETING CHANNELS ARE THEY USING?	ANALYZE COMPETITOR STRATEGIES AND IDENTIFY OPPORTUNITIES TO LEVERAGE UNDERUTILIZED OR EMERGING CHANNELS.	COMPETITOR ANALYSIS TOOLS (SPYFU, SEMRUSH), SOCIAL MEDIA MONITORING TOOLS, INDUSTRY REPORTS
	2. ARE THERE ANY UNTAPPED OR OVERLOOKED MARKETING CHANNELS THAT MY COMPETITORS ARE NOT UTILIZING?	EXPLORE ALTERNATIVE CHANNELS OR APPROACHES TO DIFFERENTIATE YOUR BRAND FROM COMPETITORS.	EMERGING SOCIAL MEDIA PLATFORMS (CLUBHOUSE, TIKTOK), NICHE INDUSTRY PUBLICATIONS, LOCAL ADVERTISING OPPORTUNITIES
CREATIVITY & INNOVATION	1. AM I OPEN TO TRYING NEW AND INNOVATIVE MARKETING CHANNELS?	CONSIDER EXPERIMENTING WITH UNCONVENTIONAL CHANNELS TO STAND OUT AND CAPTURE AUDIENCE ATTENTION.	VIRTUAL REALITY EXPERIENCES, INTERACTIVE CONTENT (QUIZZES, POLLS), AUGMENTED REALITY ADVERTISING, EXPERIENTIAL MARKETING EVENTS
	2. HOW CAN I DIFFERENTIATE MY BRAND BY LEVERAGING UNCONVENTIONAL MARKETING CHANNELS?	LOOK FOR CREATIVE WAYS TO USE NON-TRADITIONAL CHANNELS THAT ALIGN WITH YOUR BRAND IDENTITY AND RESONATE WITH YOUR AUDIENCE.	VR EXPERIENCES FOR TECH BRANDS, INTERACTIVE POLLS FOR ENGAGEMENT, AR FILTERS ON SOCIAL MEDIA, BRANDED POP-UP EVENTS

EVALUATING YOUR STRATEGY

WHICH CHANNELS ARE YOU CURRENTLY USING TO DISTRIBUTE YOUR CONTENT?

LIST THE CHANNELS YOU ARE ACTIVELY USING (E.G., SOCIAL MEDIA PLATFORMS, EMAIL, BLOGS, VIDEO PLATFORMS).

IS YOUR CONTENT TAILORED TO EACH PLATFORM?

THINK ABOUT HOW YOUR CONTENT IS OPTIMIZED FOR EACH CHANNEL. DOES YOUR INSTAGRAM CONTENT DIFFER FROM YOUR LINKEDIN POSTS? ARE YOU USING THE STRENGTHS OF EACH PLATFORM EFFECTIVELY?

WHAT'S WORKING WELL, AND WHAT ISN'T?

BASED ON YOUR CURRENT PERFORMANCE, WHICH CHANNELS ARE DELIVERING THE BEST RESULTS? WHERE COULD YOU IMPROVE? CONSIDER THINGS LIKE ENGAGEMENT, CONVERSION, AND REACH.

WHAT CHANNELS COULD YOU ADD OR REMOVE FROM YOUR STRATEGY?

ARE THERE ANY NEW PLATFORMS OR TOOLS YOU SHOULD EXPLORE? OR ARE THERE ANY CHANNELS YOU SHOULD STOP USING BECAUSE THEY AREN'T ALIGNED WITH YOUR GOALS?

WHAT'S ONE CHANGE YOU'D MAKE TO OPTIMIZE YOUR MULTI-CHANNEL APPROACH?

WHETHER IT'S ADJUSTING TIMING, REPURPOSING CONTENT, OR IMPROVING CONSISTENCY ACROSS PLATFORMS, WRITE DOWN ONE ACTIONABLE CHANGE YOU CAN MAKE RIGHT NOW TO ENHANCE YOUR CONTENT DISTRIBUTION.

CONTENT PLANNER

CAMPAIGN MANAGER

CAMPAIGN NAME

DATE START:

DATE END:

TOTAL DAYS:

DAILY BUDGET:

BUDGET IN TOTAL:

PLATFORM:

DESCRIPTION

- [ ] PROMOTING (NEW) PRODUCT
- [ ] INCREASE WEBSITE TRAFFIC
- [ ] GAIN LIKES AND FOLLOWERS
- [ ] GIVEAWAY CAMPAIGN
- [ ] PROMOTE NEW BLOG OR PODCAST
- [ ] INCREASE VISIBILITY
- [ ] ATTRACT NEW CUSTOMERS
- [ ]
- [ ]
- [ ]

TARGET AUDIENCE

GENDER

AGE RANGE

LOCATION

MARTIAL STATUS

INCOME

INTERESTS

BUSINESS

PRIVATE

HASHTAG LIST

#

#

#

#

#

#

#

RESULTS

SUCCESS RATE ☆☆☆☆☆

REVENUE EARNED

LINK CLICKS

LIKES

COMMENTS

PROFILE VIEWS

RECOMMENDATIONS

CONTENT PLANNER

GIVEAWAY TRACKER

SPONSOR:

ITEM(S):

DATE START: DATE END: NO. OF ENTRIES:

RULES OF ENTRY

SOCIAL MEDIA PROMOTION

☐ INSTAGRAM ☐ PINTEREST ☐ FACEBOOK ☐ TWITTER ☐ YOUTUBE ☐ ____________ ☐ ____________

WINNER:

WINNER E-MAIL:

ANNOUNCEMENT DATE: WINNER NOTIFIED ☐ ITEM SEND ☐

GIVEAWAY RULES

INSTRUCTIONS

4

STOP SCROLLING

FROM NOISE TO SIGNAL

CHAPTER IV.
STOP SCROLLING

STAND OUT WITH CONTENT THAT ENGAGES

CRAFTING COMPELLING HEADLINES AND SUBJECT LINES

Crafting compelling headlines and subject lines is essential for capturing the attention of your audience amidst the sea of content vying for their attention. In today's fast-paced digital landscape, people are bombarded with information on a constant basis—emails, social media updates, advertisements, blog posts, and so much more. Your headline or subject line serves as the gateway to your content, enticing readers to click and engage further. It's your first chance to make an impression, and it can make or break the effectiveness of your content.

To create headlines or subject lines that grab attention, start by keeping them concise and clear. Aim for brevity, as long-winded titles or subject lines can get lost in the shuffle. At the same time, make sure they convey the value of what's inside. Don't just tell readers what your content is about—give them a reason to care. Offer a glimpse of the benefit or insight they'll gain by clicking through. You want them to feel like they're missing out if they don't engage.

Incorporating power words, questions, or numbers is a proven strategy to pique curiosity and spark interest. Words like "unlock," "discover," or "transform" invoke a sense of potential and promise. Similarly, numbers can add clarity and specificity to your headline, creating intrigue. Think about how you respond when you see a list of "5 ways" or "7 tips"—they often stand out because they offer structured, digestible information.

Questions are another fantastic way to make your headlines more engaging. A question naturally invites curiosity, prompting readers to seek out the answer. For example, a headline like, "Are you making these common marketing mistakes?" entices readers to click to find out more.

Experiment with different formats and styles to see what resonates best with your audience. You might discover that more casual, conversational tones work better for some campaigns, while others might require a more formal approach. Testing is key—whether it's through A/B testing or simply tracking open rates and engagement levels, you'll be able to fine-tune your approach based on the results.

One time I had to draft an email to a company's entire commercial organization (a few thousand people) and try to capture their attention about how the company was updating and standardizing the Statements of Work (SOWs) process. Doesn't sound like a very fun topic— I know. But, the work that was being done to update and standardize this process would make the commercial team's life much easier and more efficient, and will, in turn, create happier customers. All in all, it was good news for them, but the topic is a bit dry. So, I took a risk and wrote an attention-grabbing headline, "I've got 99 problems and an SOW is one!" and then followed the same humorous and casual tone throughout the body of the message. The results? A 90% open rate! That was a massive jump from the average 35% for commercial organization email open rates.

Having fun and investing time in creativity when you write your headlines or subject lines makes a difference. It can be the difference between clicking to open that email or picking up your book or leaving it to gather dust on the digital or bookstore shelf. People are drawn to content that stands out and feels authentic, so don't be afraid to experiment and take some risks with your messaging.

DESIGN PRINCIPLES FOR VISUAL CONTENT

In the visually-driven world of digital media, leveraging design principles is essential for creating content that catches the eye and captivates the audience. Whether it's images, infographics, or videos, visual content should be visually appealing, easy to digest, and aligned with your brand's aesthetic. When designed well, visuals can convey complex ideas in a way that's easy to understand and emotionally engaging. They help break up text-heavy content, making it more accessible and shareable.

Pay attention to factors like color, typography, and composition to create a cohesive and visually stunning experience. Colors play a powerful role in influencing mood and perception, so choose a palette that reflects your brand's identity and evokes the right emotions. For instance, blue is often associated with trust and professionalism, while green can represent growth and sustainability. Typography should be clear and legible, with a mix of fonts that complement each other without overwhelming the reader. Keep your compositions balanced and uncluttered—too much visual noise can overwhelm the viewer and distract from your message.

Also, keep in mind the preferences and browsing habits of your audience when designing visual content. Mobile optimization is crucial, as more people than ever are consuming content on their smartphones and tablets. Ensure that your visuals are responsive, meaning they adjust and display correctly on all device sizes. Accessibility is equally important—use alt text for images, ensure sufficient color contrast for readability, and consider other accessibility guidelines to make your content available to everyone. By prioritizing visual storytelling, you can enhance the effectiveness of your content and leave a lasting impression on your audience.

When done right, design principles can elevate your content and make it more engaging. Visuals are not just decorative—they should work hand in hand with your messaging to reinforce your brand identity, convey your values, and inspire action. The way you design your content can shape how your audience perceives your brand and increase the chances they'll share it with others.

THE POWER OF COLOR IN BRANDING AND CONTENT CREATION

Color is one of the most powerful tools in design, capable of influencing emotions, shaping perceptions, and driving consumer behavior. In branding and content creation, color is far more than just an aesthetic choice—it plays a psychological role in how your audience interacts with your brand and how they interpret your messaging. Understanding the power of color can help you craft more impactful, memorable content that resonates with your audience on a deeper level.

EMOTIONAL IMPACT OF COLOR

Each color carries with it certain associations and emotions. These associations are often cultural, psychological, and instinctual, and they can vary depending on the context in which they are used. For example, blue is often associated with calmness, trust, and professionalism, which is why many corporate brands use blue in their logos and designs. Red, on the other hand, is a color that evokes excitement, passion, and urgency, which is why it's commonly used in call-to-action buttons or clearance sales.

USING COLOR STRATEGICALLY IN YOUR BRAND

The colors you choose for your branding—whether it's for your logo, website, social media graphics, or advertising materials—can help create the perception you want for your business. If your brand is meant to be seen as innovative and cutting-edge, using bold colors like red or electric blue can communicate that message effectively. On the other hand, if your brand is focused on sustainability or wellness, you might want to use shades of green or earth tones to convey those values.

WHEN CHOOSING COLORS, CONSIDER THE FOLLOWING FACTORS:

- **BRAND IDENTITY:** What values and emotions do you want your brand to represent? Think about how you want your audience to feel when they interact with your brand. If your brand is about trust and reliability, blue might be your best choice. If you want to evoke energy and excitement, consider red or orange.
- **AUDIENCE DEMOGRAPHICS:** Your target audience's cultural background, age, gender, and preferences can all influence how they perceive color. For example, younger consumers may be more drawn to bright, bold colors, while older audiences may appreciate more muted, traditional tones.
- **CULTURAL SIGNIFICANCE:** Keep in mind that color meanings can vary widely across cultures. For example, white is often associated with purity in Western cultures, but it is also linked to mourning in some Eastern cultures. Understanding these differences can help ensure that your brand resonates with a global audience.
- **COLOR COMBINATIONS:** It's not just about individual colors—how colors work together can influence the overall feel of your brand. Complementary colors (opposite each other on the color wheel) like blue and orange create contrast and can draw attention, while analogous colors (next to each other on the wheel) like blue and green are more calming and harmonious. Make sure your color palette is balanced and consistent across all brand touchpoints.

COLOR IN DIGITAL AND PRINT DESIGN

Color plays a significant role in both digital and print content, but there are different considerations for each medium. On digital platforms, colors may look different depending on the screen resolution and settings. That's why it's important to test how your colors appear on various devices and browsers to ensure they convey the right message and feel.

In print design, colors are influenced by the printing process and materials used. CMYK (cyan, magenta, yellow, black) is the color model used for printing, and it differs from the RGB (red, green, blue) model used for digital screens. It's essential to work with your printer to ensure your colors are consistent in both digital and print materials.

THE SUBTLETY OF COLOR CONTRAST AND ACCESSIBILITY

Color contrast isn't just an aesthetic consideration—it's an accessibility one as well. Ensuring that your content is easily readable by everyone, including people with visual impairments or color blindness, is crucial. High contrast between text and background (such as dark text on a light background) enhances readability, while poor contrast (like light grey text on a white background) can make your content difficult to engage with.

Consider using tools like the WebAIM Contrast Checker to ensure your designs meet accessibility standards and can be read by as many people as possible.

COLOR AND BRAND RECOGNITION

The colors you choose can have a lasting impact on your brand recognition. Think about the big brands that come to mind when you think of specific colors. Color plays a pivotal role in brand recall, helping to create an association between the color and the product or service.

By selecting the right color palette and using it consistently across all touchpoints, you can enhance brand recognition and create a stronger connection with your audience.

THE POWER OF COLOR

The power of color in branding and content creation is undeniable. It influences emotions, guides consumer behavior, and can make your content stand out in a crowded digital space. When used thoughtfully and strategically, color can elevate your brand's message, foster emotional connections with your audience, and increase the effectiveness of your marketing efforts. By understanding the psychological impact of color, aligning it with your brand identity, and using it consistently, you'll be able to create a visually compelling experience that resonates with your audience and strengthens your brand's presence.

INCORPORATING MULTIMEDIA ELEMENTS

Incorporating multimedia elements effectively is key to creating dynamic and engaging content experiences for your audience. From videos and podcasts to interactive graphics and animations, multimedia content allows you to convey information in diverse and compelling ways. This makes your content more engaging and helps to maintain your audience's attention for longer periods of time.

Consider the preferences and consumption habits of your audience when selecting multimedia formats. If your audience is primarily on the go, podcasts might be an excellent choice for delivering valuable content in a way that's easy to consume while multitasking. For audiences that prefer visuals, videos can be used to convey product demos, tutorials, or storytelling elements that are far more effective than text alone. Interactive graphics, polls, and quizzes provide fun, immersive ways to keep users engaged while simultaneously collecting data about their preferences.

Leverage multimedia to enhance storytelling, demonstrate products or services, or provide valuable insights and entertainment. Videos, for example, can show rather than tell, allowing your audience to see your products in action, hear testimonials, or experience your brand story in a more personal, emotional way. Infographics condense complex information into easily digestible visuals, making it easier for people to understand and retain important data.

Remember to optimize your multimedia content for different platforms and devices to reach the widest possible audience. Videos should be formatted for mobile viewing and social media platforms, and podcasts should be accessible through popular channels like Apple Podcasts or Spotify. Additionally, make sure that your multimedia content loads quickly and is compatible with various internet speeds to avoid frustrating your audience.

By embracing the power of multimedia, you can elevate your content and make a memorable impact on your audience. Multimedia elements add depth to your messaging, provide variety in how information is presented, and enhance the user experience. The more engaging and interactive your content is, the more likely your audience will engage with it, share it, and return for more.

Incorporating diverse content types into your overall content strategy isn't just about creating variety—it's about responding to the different ways people consume information and finding the most effective ways to connect with them. By offering a mix of multimedia content, you'll keep your audience engaged, reach them on a deeper level, and increase your chances of achieving your business goals.

VISUAL ELEMENTS

MEANING OF COLOR

YELLOW	ORANGE	RED
FRIENDLY, CHEERFUL, YOUTHFUL, ENERGY, POSITIVITY HAPPINESS	ENERGY, EXCITEMENT, PROSPERITY, WARMTH, PLAYFULNESS, CHANGE	GENTLENESS, ENERGY, WARMTH, LOVE, COMFORT
MAGENTA	**PURPLE**	**BLUE**
PHYSICAL TRANQUILITY, WARMTH, LOVE	WISDOM, LUXURY, WEALTH, SPIRITUALITY, IMAGINATIVE, SOPHISTICATION	TRUST, LOYALITY, DEPENDABILITY, LOGIC, SERENITY, SECURITY, SAFETY
TURQUOISE	**GREEN**	**BROWN**
COMMUNICATION, CLARITY, CALMNESS, INSPIRATION, EXPRESSION, HEALING	HEALTH, HOPE, FRESHNESS, NATURE, GROWTH, PROSPERITY, OPTIMISM	SERIOUSNESS, WARMTH, RELIABILITY, SUPPORT, AUTHENTICITY
BLACK	**GRAY**	**WHITE**
SOPHISTICATION, SECURITY, POWER, ELEGANCE, AUTHORITY, SUBSTANCE	TIMELESSNESS, NEUTRALITY, RELIABILITY, BALANCE, INTELLIGENCE, STRENGTH	CLARITY, SIMPLICITY, SOPHISTICATION

5 VISUAL BRAND ESSENTIALS

1. YOUR BRAND LOGO OR WORDMARK

YOUR BRAND'S UNIQUE SIGNIFIER IS YOUR IDENTITY IN ITS SIMPLEST FORM. IT SHOULD IMMEDIATELY CALL TO MIND YOUR ORGANIZATION — AND (AS IMPORTANTLY) CALL TO HEART THE DISTINCT EMOTIONAL APPEAL AT YOUR BRAND'S CORE. HOWEVER SIMPLE THEY APPEAR, LOGOS ARE PAINSTAKINGLY THOUGHT OUT AND STRATEGICALLY DESIGNED, REFINED AND REVISED MANY TIMES IN THE DESIGN PROCESS.

2. BRAND COLOR PALETTE

WHEN CHOOSING YOUR COLOR PALETTE, THINK CAREFULLY WHAT EMOTIONS YOU WANT TO EVOKE, WHAT AUDIENCES YOU'RE ADDRESSING AND ALL YOUR NEEDS: WEBSITE AND ONLINE SOCIAL PRESENCE; CORPORATE, EMPLOYEE AND INVESTOR COMMUNICATIONS; REPORTS, BROCHURES, SALES TOOLS AND PRESENTATIONS AS WELL AS PRINT MATERIALS.

3. CORPORATE TYPEFACES

A BRAND LOGO DEPENDS A LOT ON THE TYPEFACE YOU CHOOSE. FONT CLASSIFICATIONS ARE EXTENSIVE, SO YOUR CHOICES BECOME ENDLESS WHEN WORKING ON BRAND DEVELOPMENT. A GOOD FONT CHOICE WILL CONNECT WITH YOUR AUDIENCE ON MANY LEVELS AND WILL COMMUNICATE A CERTAIN PERSONALITY.

4. STANDARD TYPOGRAPHIC TREATMENTS

YOUR TYPOGRAPHIC IDENTITY SHOULD INCLUDE WAYS OF HANDLING KEY TYPES OF TEXT, ESPECIALLY YOUR TAGLINE OR YOUR ADDRESS. DEVELOPING A CONSISTENT WAY OF WRITING AND STYLING HEADLINES OR PULL-OUT TEXT REALLY BEGINS TO CREATE A DISTINCT VOICE FOR YOUR BRAND. WORK TO MAKE THESE SIMILAR FROM ONE APPLICATION TO THE NEXT.

5. CONSISTENT STYLE FOR IMAGES

IT'S CRUCIAL TO USE PHOTOS THAT HAVE THE SAME LOOK AND FEEL, NO MATTER WHAT IT IS. LIGHT AND AIRY, MOODY OR BOLD/COLORFUL ARE JUST A FEW EXAMPLES. AS LONG AS THEY LOOK SIMILAR AND ARE USED CONSISTENTLY, YOU ARE IN GOOD SHAPE. YOU CAN USE STOCK PHOTOS, BUT I REALLY CONSIDER INVESTING IN SOME BRAND PHOTOS, SO THAT YOU HAVE A COLLECTION OF IMAGES UNIQUE TO YOU.

5

CRACKING THE CODE: SEO AND SOCIAL

FROM NOISE TO SIGNAL

CHAPTER V.
CRACKING THE CODE

MASTER THE DIGITAL LANDSCAPE WITH STRATEGIES THAT GET RESULTS

Understanding the basics of Search Engine Optimization (SEO) is essential for ensuring that your content gets discovered by your target audience. SEO involves optimizing your content to rank higher in search engine results pages (SERPs) for relevant keywords and phrases. Start by conducting keyword research to identify the terms and phrases your audience is searching for.

Incorporate these keywords strategically into your content, including headings, meta descriptions, and alt text for images. Focus on creating high-quality, valuable content that addresses the needs and interests of your audience, as search engines prioritize relevance and user experience. By implementing SEO best practices, you can increase your visibility and attract more organic traffic to your website.

LAYING THE FOUNDATION

Start with keyword research. This is the foundation of SEO because it helps you understand what terms and phrases your audience is actually searching for. Tools like Google Keyword Planner, Ahrefs, or SEMrush can help you discover high-volume keywords in your industry, but it's not just about choosing the most popular terms. You also need to consider long-tail keywords—more specific phrases that might not have as much search volume but are highly targeted.

For example, if you sell handmade jewelry, a general keyword like "jewelry" will be highly competitive. However, a long-tail keyword like "handmade silver necklaces for women" is more specific, has less competition, and will likely attract more qualified traffic to your website. The goal is to target keywords that are relevant, specific, and likely to convert into actual customers.

Once you have a solid list of keywords, strategically incorporate them into your content. This includes titles, headings, meta descriptions, and alt text for images. But don't overstuff—search engines have become sophisticated, and they penalize content that uses excessive or unnatural keyword repetition. Instead, focus on creating high-quality, valuable content that naturally integrates your chosen keywords.

ON-PAGE SEO: OPTIMIZING CONTENT FOR SEARCH ENGINES AND USERS

On-page SEO refers to all the elements you can control on your own website to improve its search engine rankings. This includes everything from the structure of your URLs to the content you publish, and even how you organize your website.

HERE ARE SOME KEY ASPECTS TO FOCUS ON:

- **CONTENT QUALITY:** Search engines prioritize high-quality, informative content. When you create content, think about what questions your audience is asking and how your content can provide answers. Create blog posts, guides, FAQs, or videos that are comprehensive and valuable to your audience. Content that truly serves the user is more likely to be shared and linked to, which boosts its SEO.
- **HEADINGS AND SUBHEADINGS:** Use headings (H1, H2, H3, etc.) to organize your content and make it easy for readers to scan. These also help search engines understand the structure of your content. Your primary keyword should be in your H1 heading, and your secondary keywords should appear in subheadings.
- **META DESCRIPTIONS:** These short snippets appear under your page title in search results. Although meta descriptions don't directly affect SEO rankings, they influence whether people click on your page. Write compelling, concise meta descriptions that summarize the page's content while incorporating keywords.
- **ALT TEXT FOR IMAGES:** Search engines can't "see" images, but they can read the alt text. Including relevant keywords in your image descriptions helps boost SEO, especially for image-based searches. Plus, well-optimized images contribute to a better user experience, which Google prioritizes.

OFF-PAGE SEO

Off-page SEO refers to actions you can take outside of your website to impact your search engine rankings. The most important factor in off-page SEO is backlinks—links from other reputable websites to yours. Search engines view backlinks as votes of confidence for your content, indicating that other credible sources find your content valuable. The more high-quality backlinks you have, the higher your page will rank.

To build backlinks, focus on creating valuable content that people naturally want to share. You can also reach out to other websites in your industry for guest posting opportunities or to request inclusion in relevant directories or resource lists. Building relationships with industry influencers can also help amplify your brand's authority and increase the chances of getting valuable backlinks.

STRATEGIES FOR ENGAGEMENT AND GROWTH

In the fast-paced world of social media, building engagement and fostering growth requires a strategic approach. It's easy to get overwhelmed with the sheer number of platforms available, but remember that quality always trumps quantity. Start by identifying where your audience is most active. Are they engaging on Facebook, Instagram, LinkedIn, or X? Once you've identified the best platforms for your audience, tailor your content to match the unique features and audience expectations of each platform.

- **CREATING PLATFORM-SPECIFIC CONTENT:** What works on Facebook might not work on Instagram, and vice versa. For example, Instagram thrives on visuals, so posting beautiful photos or short videos is essential. On LinkedIn, longer-form articles and thought leadership pieces are more effective. Understand the nuances of each platform and create content that aligns with its strengths.
- **ENGAGEMENT THROUGH INTERACTION:** Social media isn't just about broadcasting your message; it's about building relationships. Respond to comments, ask questions, initiate conversations, and acknowledge your followers. Engagement helps foster a loyal community and keeps your audience coming back.
- **HASHTAGS AND TRENDS:** Hashtags are an important tool for increasing the visibility of your posts. Research relevant hashtags in your industry, and use them strategically to categorize your content and reach a wider audience. Don't overload your posts with hashtags, but find a few key ones that will help extend your reach. Additionally, stay on top of trending topics and incorporate them into your content when relevant.
- **CONSISTENCY AND FREQUENCY:** Regularly posting on social media keeps your brand top-of-mind for your audience. Create a content calendar to help you stay organized and maintain a consistent posting schedule. However, avoid posting for the sake of posting—each piece of content should serve a purpose and provide value.

LEVERAGING KEYWORDS AND HASHTAGS

Both SEO and social media thrive on the strategic use of keywords and hashtags. By conducting keyword research, you can identify relevant terms that align with your content and target audience. For SEO, incorporate these keywords naturally throughout your website, blog posts, and product descriptions. For social media, hashtags act as a form of categorization, helping people find your content when they search for specific topics.

On platforms like Instagram or Twitter, hashtags are an easy way to increase discoverability. Research trending hashtags or create your own branded hashtag that encourages user-generated content. Keep in mind that social media platforms have different hashtag norms—Instagram posts, for instance, can include up to 30 hashtags, but studies suggest that 7-10 hashtags tend to yield the best results.

For example, if you're a local coffee shop, you could use hashtags like #localcoffee, #coffeetime, or #coffeelover to reach a wider audience in your community or among coffee enthusiasts. Similarly, if your blog focuses on healthy living, hashtags like #healthylifestyle, #nutritiontips, and #fitnessjourney can increase your visibility to people searching for health-related content.

PUTTING IT ALL TOGETHER

The relationship between SEO and social media is complementary—each enhances the other. While SEO helps you optimize your content to rank well on search engines, social media allows you to expand your reach, engage with your audience, and drive traffic back to your website. By integrating both strategies, you can create a comprehensive digital marketing approach that increases visibility, builds brand awareness, and drives meaningful interactions with your audience.

Start by mastering the basics of SEO and understanding how search engines evaluate content. Then, use social media to amplify your message, engage with followers, and drive traffic to your site. By leveraging both SEO and social media, you'll ensure that your content is seen by more people, creating more opportunities to grow your business.

KEYWORD RESEARCH

Determine what topics you want to rank for in the search engines. You can look at what your competition is ranking for and with what content to give yourself a head start. Think of what people looking for your product/service are searching for in Google? What do they want to know? What problems are they looking to solve?

MAKE A LIST OF TOPICS THAT ARE RELATED TO YOUR NICHE AND RELEVANT FOR YOUR AUDIENCE

For the next section write down some keywords related to the above topics. You can do this by typing the topics (also try adding questions such as how, what etc)in google search box and then let google autocomplete the sentence (these are some high volume keywords that you can use). You can also search for a certain keyword and then scroll down to "related searches" for more ideas. Or you can use google keyword planner. Aim for the long tail keywords (3+ words)

MAKE A LIST OF KEYWORDS RELATED TO YOUR SERVICE/PRODUCT

THE KEYWORD TREE

This is a worksheet for braindstorming lots of relevant long tail keywords & topics (or questions that people search for) related to your specific niche. Use google keyword tool, google autofill, relevant searches, competitor's content and quora questions as your guide.

6

THE ART OF ITERATION

FROM NOISE TO SIGNAL

CHAPTER VI.
THE ART OF ITERATION

DATA-DRIVEN DECISIONS THAT EVOLVE YOUR STRATEGY AND DRIVE SUCCESS

KEEP EVOLVING FOR BETTER RESULTS (AND AVOID THE PAIN OF STAGNATION)

If you're a small business owner looking to optimize your content strategy, there's one thing you absolutely can't afford to overlook—analytics. It's like that honest friend who tells you when you have spinach in your teeth. It might sting a little, but you're better off knowing than not. In the world of content creation, analytics offer invaluable insights that help you understand how well your content is performing, where it's hitting the mark, and where it's falling flat. Without them, you're essentially driving in the dark. So, let's talk about how you can use the numbers to your advantage, refine your strategy, and ultimately get the results you're after.

WHY ANALYTICS MATTER

For small business owners, especially those wearing multiple hats (as many do), it's easy to focus on the creative side of things—writing engaging blog posts, crafting social media updates, and producing videos that you hope will go viral. But if you're not measuring how those efforts are performing, it's like cooking dinner without tasting it. Sure, you might get something edible, but is it a Michelin-star meal? Probably not.

Analytics are the secret sauce to understanding what's actually happening with your content. They give you a clear picture of how your audience is interacting with your brand. Are they clicking through to your website? Are they spending more time reading your posts or just skimming and bouncing? Are they converting into customers? These are the questions analytics help answer, and once you have those answers, you can fine-tune your strategy for maximum impact. It's about making data-informed decisions that align with your business goals. After all, you don't want to just guess what works—you want to know.

KEY METRICS TO TRACK AND ANALYZE

Understanding which key metrics to track and analyze is essential for extracting actionable insights from your content performance data. To get started, think of metrics as your personal content fitness tracker. Just like tracking your steps or calories burned, tracking content metrics helps you measure progress. But instead of measuring how many steps you've taken, you're measuring how much attention your audience is giving you. Let's dive into some of the key metrics you should keep your eyes on:

- **WEBSITE TRAFFIC:** This is the big one. Are people finding your content? Traffic shows how many people are visiting your site, and it's a good indicator of whether your SEO, social media, and other promotional strategies are working. If traffic is low, it could signal that your content isn't being discovered or is being buried by the competition.
- **ENGAGEMENT RATES:** Engagement is the holy grail of content success. It's not enough just to drive traffic to your site—you want people interacting with your content. Engagement metrics like click-through rates (CTR), time spent on page, comments, shares, and likes can tell you whether people are actually consuming and engaging with your content. If engagement is high, your content is resonating. If it's low, maybe it's time to tweak your approach.
- **CONVERSION RATES:** Now, here's where the rubber meets the road. Conversions tell you how many visitors are taking the desired action—whether it's signing up for your newsletter, making a purchase, or downloading a resource. High conversion rates are the gold standard, as they directly translate into business growth. If your traffic is high but conversions are low, you need to dig deeper to see where the bottleneck is—maybe your calls-to-action need to be more compelling or your landing pages need optimizing.
- **RETURN ON INVESTMENT (ROI):** Of course, as a small business owner, your bottom line matters. ROI measures the effectiveness of your marketing efforts by comparing the revenue generated from content against the costs of producing and promoting that content. If you're not measuring ROI, you're essentially flying blind. Don't just throw content out there and hope for the best—know what's driving results and make sure your efforts are yielding positive returns.
- **AUDIENCE DEMOGRAPHICS & BEHAVIOR:** Knowing who your audience is—and how they behave—can help you create better, more targeted content. Dive into your audience's age, location, interests, and browsing behaviors to uncover trends. Are your followers mostly 18-24-year-olds on Instagram, or

are they business professionals browsing LinkedIn? Use this information to tailor your content more precisely to your audience's preferences.

ITERATIVE IMPROVEMENTS BASED ON DATA-DRIVEN INSIGHTS

Here's the deal: iteration is everything. If you're not evolving based on data, you're stuck in a loop of doing the same things over and over, hoping for different results (sound familiar?). The beauty of analytics is that they provide feedback that can be used to fine-tune and improve your content strategy. Think of it like having a GPS for your business: it shows you where you are, where you're going, and what adjustments you need to make to get there faster.

LET'S BREAK THIS DOWN A BIT:

- **EXPERIMENT WITH CONTENT FORMATS:** Just like fashion trends, content formats change over time. What worked six months ago may no longer be effective. Test different content formats to see what resonates best with your audience. If blog posts are getting a lot of engagement but your videos are falling flat, try a hybrid approach—integrate video snippets within your written content, or experiment with longer-form video content to see if your audience is craving more visual storytelling.
- **TEST DIFFERENT TOPICS:** Sometimes, it's not the format that's the problem—it's the topic. Dive into your analytics and identify which topics your audience is most interested in. Have your "how-to" guides been getting a lot of traffic? Are your thought leadership posts sparking discussions? Use this data to test new content ideas and see what your audience reacts to. Don't be afraid to explore new angles, but always keep your core audience in mind.
- **REFINING HEADLINES, VISUALS, AND CTAS:** Even small tweaks can make a huge difference. A slight change to your headline can lead to a better click-through rate. Try out different variations, keeping track of what works. The same goes for visuals and calls-to-action (CTAs). A button that says "Buy Now" might convert better than one that says "Shop Here." Experiment with different wording, colors, and placements to optimize performance.
- **A/B TESTING:** Think of A/B testing like a science experiment for your content. You take two variations of the same content—whether it's a blog post, an email, or a landing page—and test them against each other to see which one performs better. This is a great way to fine-tune headlines, imagery, or even the length of your content. The more you test, the more insights you gain into your audience's preferences, and the better you can optimize your strategy.

- **MEASURE, ADJUST, REPEAT:** Just like working out at the gym, content iteration is all about consistency. You'll never reach your peak performance after one test or adjustment. Keep tracking metrics, adjusting your content, and measuring your results. The key is to stay flexible and open to change, so you can keep improving over time.

ITERATE LIKE A PRO (AND BE PREPARED TO PIVOT)

In the world of content creation, there's always room for improvement. The beauty of a data-driven approach is that you can continually refine your strategy, stay agile, and pivot when necessary. The more you embrace iteration, the more you set yourself up for long-term success. So, don't be afraid to make mistakes, experiment, and use those valuable insights to fine-tune your approach. It's not about being perfect from the start—it's about getting better, one step at a time. After all, perfection is overrated. The real magic happens when you embrace the process of iteration and let your data guide you toward continuous improvement.

WORKBOOK EXERCISE: ANALYZING AND ITERATING YOUR CONTENT STRATEGY

Now that you're armed with the basics, it's time to put it all into action. Use this workbook exercise to analyze your content performance and identify areas for iteration. Take a deep dive into your analytics, track your key metrics, and experiment with new strategies to see how your content can evolve. With each iteration, you'll be one step closer to mastering the art of content creation and driving better results for your business.

Remember, in the world of content strategy, the only thing that's constant is change. Keep iterating, stay curious, and watch your business grow.

TAKING STOCK

ANNUAL TRACKER

DO A REVIEW OF LAST YEAR'S DATA

PLATFORM

☐ ☐ ☐ ☐ ☐ ☐ ☐ ☐ ______

YEAR

NOTES

MONTH	FOLLOWERS	GROWTH	POSTS	TOP VIEWED
JANUARY				
FEBRUARY				
MARCH				
APRIL				
MAY				
JUNE				
JULY				
AUGUST				
SEPTEMBER				
OCTOBER				
NOVEMBER				
DECEMBER				

TAKING STOCK

ANNUAL TRACKER

START TRACKING THIS YEAR'S DATA

PLATFORM

☐ ☐ ☐ ☐ ☐ ☐ ☐ ☐ ____

YEAR

NOTES

MONTH	FOLLOWERS	GROWTH	POSTS	TOP VIEWED
JANUARY				
FEBRUARY				
MARCH				
APRIL				
MAY				
JUNE				
JULY				
AUGUST				
SEPTEMBER				
OCTOBER				
NOVEMBER				
DECEMBER				

TRACK YOUR KEY METRICS

This activity will help you evaluate the performance of your content, understand what's working, and refine your approach.

You will focus on three key steps: tracking metrics, analyzing your audience, and making changes based on insights.

IDENTIFY YOUR BUSINESS GOAL

WHAT IS YOUR PRIMARY BUSINESS GOAL RIGHT NOW?

EXAMPLE:
INCREASE WEBSITE TRAFFIC BY 15% OVER THE NEXT THREE MONTHS.

CHOOSE YOUR METRICS

PICK 3 KEY METRICS TO TRACK THAT ALIGN WITH YOUR GOAL.

EXAMPLE:

- WEBSITE TRAFFIC
- CONVERSION RATES
- SOCIAL MEDIA ENGAGEMENT (LIKES, SHARES, COMMENTS)

SET YOUR TARGET

SET A REALISTIC TARGET FOR EACH OF THE METRICS YOU'VE CHOSEN.

EXAMPLE:

- WEBSITE TRAFFIC: 12,000 VISITS PER MONTH
- CONVERSION RATE: 3%
- SOCIAL MEDIA ENGAGEMENT: 6% ENGAGEMENT RATE

ANALYZE AUDIENCE BEHAVIOR

This activity will help you evaluate the performance of your content, understand what's working, and refine your approach.

You will focus on three key steps: tracking metrics, analyzing your audience, and making changes based on insights.

UNDERSTAND YOUR AUDIENCE

REVIEW DATA ON WHO YOUR AUDIENCE IS. YOU CAN FIND THIS DATA IN YOUR ANALYTICS TOOLS.

EXAMPLE:
AUDIENCE IS MOSTLY 25-34 YEARS OLD, BASED IN URBAN AREAS, AND INTERESTED IN HEALTH AND WELLNESS.

REVIEW ENGAGEMENT

LOOK AT HOW YOUR AUDIENCE IS ENGAGING WITH YOUR CONTENT. ARE THEY STAYING ON YOUR SITE? ARE THEY INTERACTING WITH YOUR SOCIAL MEDIA POSTS?

EXAMPLE:

- HIGH ENGAGEMENT WITH BLOG POSTS (COMMENTS AND SHARES).
- LOW ENGAGEMENT ON INSTAGRAM POSTS.

MAKE ADJUSTMENTS

BASED ON WHAT YOU LEARN, WHAT CAN YOU ADJUST IN YOUR CONTENT? FOR EXAMPLE, IF VIDEOS ARE GETTING MORE ENGAGEMENT, CONSIDER CREATING MORE VIDEO CONTENT.

EXAMPLE:
CREATE MORE BLOG POSTS RELATED TO WELLNESS TRENDS AND REDUCE INSTAGRAM-ONLY POSTS.

EXPERIMENT & IMPROVE

This activity will help you evaluate the performance of your content, understand what's working, and refine your approach.

You will focus on three key steps: tracking metrics, analyzing your audience, and making changes based on insights.

TRY SOMETHING NEW

PICK ONE EXPERIMENT TO TEST. FOR EXAMPLE, IF YOU THINK YOUR AUDIENCE WOULD ENGAGE MORE WITH VIDEOS, TRY POSTING VIDEOS FOR THE NEXT WEEK.

EXAMPLE:
POST ONE VIDEO PER WEEK FOR THE NEXT MONTH, FEATURING CUSTOMER TESTIMONIALS.

MEASURE THE RESULTS

TRACK THE SAME KEY METRICS (TRAFFIC, CONVERSION RATES, SOCIAL MEDIA ENGAGEMENT) TO SEE IF THE EXPERIMENT IS WORKING.

EXAMPLE:

- WEBSITE TRAFFIC INCREASED BY 10%.
- SOCIAL MEDIA ENGAGEMENT INCREASED BY 3%.

ADJUST & REPEAT

BASED ON THE RESULTS, DECIDE WHAT CHANGES TO MAKE. DID THE EXPERIMENT HELP? WILL YOU CONTINUE WITH THE CHANGE OR TRY SOMETHING ELSE?

EXAMPLE:
KEEP POSTING CUSTOMER TESTIMONIAL VIDEOS EVERY WEEK AND EXPERIMENT WITH VIDEO ADS ON SOCIAL MEDIA.

REFLECTION

At the end of these activities, reflect and ask yourself these questions to help you further iterate.

QUESTION 1

WHAT WORKED WELL IN YOUR CONTENT STRATEGY?

QUESTION 2

WHAT CAN BE IMPROVED?

QUESTION 3

WHAT WILL YOU FOCUS ON FOR YOUR NEXT CONTENT ITERATION?

NOTES :

7

STORIES THAT STICK: CASE STUDIES

CHAPTER VII. STORIES THAT STICK

WHAT WORKS, WHAT FAILS, AND WHY

REAL-WORLD EXAMPLES OF HIGH-IMPACT CONTENT CAMPAIGNS

Exploring real-world examples of high-impact content campaigns offers valuable insights and inspiration for small business owners looking to elevate their own strategies. These case studies showcase how brands across various industries have successfully captured the attention of their audience and achieved meaningful results through strategic content marketing efforts. By analyzing the tactics and techniques employed in these campaigns, you can glean actionable takeaways and apply them to your own business. Whether it's a viral social media campaign, a compelling video series, or an engaging email marketing campaign, these examples demonstrate the power of creativity, authenticity, and strategic planning in driving success.

LET'S TAKE A LOOK AT SOME STAND OUT CAMPAIGNS...

DOVE'S "REAL BEAUTY" CAMPAIGN:

Dove's "Real Beauty" campaign aimed to challenge conventional beauty standards and celebrate diverse representations of beauty. The campaign featured real women of various shapes, sizes, and ethnicities instead of models, encouraging women to embrace their natural beauty. Dove produced a series of videos, print ads, and social media content promoting body positivity and self-confidence. The campaign received widespread praise for its empowering message and generated significant social media engagement, boosting Dove's brand reputation and sales.

AIRBNB'S "LIVE THERE" CAMPAIGN:

Airbnb's "Live There" campaign focused on experiential storytelling to inspire travelers to immerse themselves in local cultures and communities while traveling. The campaign included a series of short films showcasing unique travel experiences, such as staying in a treehouse or living with a local family. Airbnb leveraged user-generated content and social media influencers to amplify the campaign's reach and authenticity. The "Live There" campaign resonated with travelers seeking authentic and meaningful experiences, contributing to Airbnb's rapid growth and market dominance.

RED BULL'S "STRATOS" SPACE JUMP:

Red Bull's "Stratos" space jump campaign was a groundbreaking event that captured global attention and generated immense brand exposure. The campaign involved Austrian skydiver Felix Baumgartner jumping from the edge of space, breaking the sound barrier during freefall. Red Bull live-streamed the event on multiple platforms, creating a thrilling and immersive experience for viewers worldwide. The "Stratos" space jump not only showcased Red Bull's commitment to extreme sports and innovation but also reinforced its brand image as a purveyor of adrenaline-fueled adventures.

NIKE'S "DREAM CRAZY" CAMPAIGN WITH COLIN KAEPERNICK:

Nike's "Dream Crazy" campaign featuring former NFL quarterback Colin Kaepernick sparked widespread controversy and conversation around social justice issues. The campaign's centerpiece was a powerful commercial narrated by Kaepernick, emphasizing the message of perseverance, ambition, and challenging the status quo. Despite facing backlash from some consumers, Nike's bold stance on social activism resonated with its target audience and received overwhelming support from younger generations and advocates for equality. The "Dream Crazy" campaign reaffirmed Nike's commitment to social responsibility and drove significant brand engagement and sales.

COCA-COLA'S "SHARE A COKE" CAMPAIGN:

Coca-Cola's "Share a Coke" campaign personalized its iconic bottles by replacing the brand name with popular first names. The campaign encouraged consumers to find and share Coke bottles with their friends and family, creating a sense of connection and emotional attachment to the brand. Coca-Cola leveraged social media and user-generated content to amplify the campaign's reach, with consumers sharing photos of personalized Coke bottles online. The "Share a Coke" campaign revitalized Coca-Cola's sales and brand relevance, becoming one of the most successful marketing initiatives in the company's history.

LEGO'S "REBUILD THE WORLD" CAMPAIGN:

LEGO's "Rebuild the World" campaign celebrated creativity and imagination by showcasing children's fantastical creations made with LEGO bricks. The campaign included a vibrant mix of videos, print ads, and social media content featuring whimsical LEGO builds and inspiring stories of young builders. LEGO encouraged consumers to share their own creations using the hashtag #RebuildTheWorld, fostering a sense of community and creativity among fans worldwide. The "Rebuild the World" campaign reinforced LEGO's brand values and drove engagement both online and offline, strengthening its position as a beloved and iconic toy brand.

These case studies help demonstrate what “good” looks like and how strategic content campaigns can effectively engage audiences, drive brand awareness, and create lasting impact in the real world. But, these big companies don’t always get it right! Let’s take a closer look at some of the biggest marketing campaign failures in recent years.

#FAIL

Here are case studies of brands that encountered challenges or faced backlash:

PEPSI'S "LIVE FOR NOW" CAMPAIGN FEATURING KENDALL JENNER:

In 2017, Pepsi launched a controversial ad featuring model Kendall Jenner participating in a protest-inspired scene where she hands a can of Pepsi to a police officer, seemingly resolving tensions and bringing unity. The ad was criticized for trivializing social justice movements like Black Lives Matter and co-opting activism for commercial gain. Pepsi faced widespread backlash on social media, with many accusing the brand of insensitivity and exploitation. Ultimately, Pepsi pulled the ad and issued an apology, acknowledging the misstep and the need to better understand complex social issues before attempting to engage with them in advertising.

MCDONALD'S #MCDSTORIES TWITTER CAMPAIGN:

In 2012, McDonald's launched the #McDStories hashtag on Twitter as part of a marketing campaign to promote its food quality and customer experience. However, the campaign backfired when users hijacked the hashtag to share negative stories and criticisms about their experiences with McDonald's, including instances of food poisoning and unsanitary conditions. The campaign quickly spiraled out of control, with negative tweets overshadowing any positive messaging McDonald's had intended. The #McDStories campaign serves as a cautionary tale about the unpredictable nature of social media and the importance of careful planning and moderation in user-generated content campaigns.

AMAZON'S FIRE PHONE LAUNCH:

Amazon's launch of the Fire Phone in 2014 was highly anticipated, but the accompanying marketing campaign failed to resonate with consumers. Despite significant investment in advertising and promotion, including Super Bowl commercials and exclusive partnerships, the Fire Phone struggled to gain traction in the competitive smartphone market. The campaign's messaging failed to clearly communicate the value proposition of the Fire Phone, leading to confusion among consumers and lackluster sales. Ultimately, Amazon discontinued the Fire Phone just over a year after its launch, resulting in a costly failure for the brand.

BURGER KING'S "SUBSERVIENT CHICKEN" CAMPAIGN:

Burger King's "Subservient Chicken" campaign in 2004 was an early example of viral marketing but ultimately failed to drive meaningful results for the brand. The campaign featured a website where users could interact with a person in a chicken costume, commanding them to perform various actions through typed commands. While the campaign generated significant buzz and website traffic, it failed to translate into increased sales or brand loyalty for Burger King. Critics argued that the campaign lacked a clear connection to Burger King's core products and failed to engage consumers beyond the novelty factor of the interactive chicken character.

GAP'S LOGO REDESIGN DEBACLE:

In 2010, Gap unveiled a new logo as part of a rebranding effort aimed at modernizing the company's image. However, the new logo received widespread criticism from consumers and design professionals alike for its perceived lack of creativity and deviation from Gap's iconic branding. The backlash was swift and intense, with many expressing disappointment and confusion over the sudden change. In response to the negative feedback, Gap reverted to its original logo within a week of the redesign, admitting that it had underestimated the emotional connection consumers had with the brand's visual identity.

NIVEA'S "WHITE IS PURITY" AD:

In 2017, Nivea faced backlash for a social media ad promoting its "Invisible for Black & White" deodorant that featured the slogan "White is Purity." The ad, which was posted on Nivea's Middle East Facebook page, was criticized for its racially insensitive messaging and perceived promotion of white supremacy. Nivea quickly removed the ad and issued an apology, stating that the campaign had not reflected the brand's values of diversity and inclusivity. The incident highlighted the importance of cultural sensitivity and thorough review processes in global marketing campaigns.

These case studies demonstrate the potential risks and pitfalls of content campaigns when brands fail to effectively resonate with their audience, misjudge cultural sensitivities, and struggle to communicate their messaging clearly. Talk about a reputation issue!

ANALYSIS OF SUCCESSFUL CONTENT STRATEGIES FROM VARIOUS INDUSTRIES

Analyzing successful content strategies from a diverse range of industries provides you, the small business owner, with valuable insights into what works and what doesn't in the ever-evolving landscape of content marketing. By examining the approaches taken by brands in industries similar to yours, you can gain a deeper understanding of the tactics and techniques that resonate most with your target audience. Look for common themes and trends across these strategies, as well as any unique insights that may be applicable to your own business. By learning from the successes and failures of others, you can refine your content strategy and increase your chances of achieving meaningful results.

LESSONS LEARNED AND ACTIONABLE TAKEAWAYS

Reflecting on the case studies and examples presented in this section offers valuable lessons and actionable takeaways for small business owners looking to improve their content marketing efforts. Consider the key strategies and tactics employed by successful brands and how they can be adapted to suit your own business goals and objectives. Whether it's the importance of storytelling, the value of authenticity, or the impact of data-driven decision-making, each example provides valuable lessons that can inform and inspire your own content strategy. By incorporating these insights into your approach, you can create more effective and impactful content that resonates with your audience and drives results for your business.

LEARNING IN ACTION

STEP 1: IDENTIFY SUCCESSFUL CAMPAIGN ELEMENTS

CAMPAIGN EXAMPLE	KEY ELEMENTS OF SUCCESS	HOW CAN YOU APPLY THIS?
DOVE'S "REAL BEAUTY"	AUTHENTICITY, EMOTIONAL APPEAL, EMPOWERING MESSAGE	HOW CAN YOU PROMOTE AUTHENTICITY OR A STRONG VALUE IN YOUR MESSAGING?
AIRBNB'S "LIVE THERE"	EXPERIENTIAL STORYTELLING, USER-GENERATED CONTENT, INFLUENCERS	HOW CAN YOU USE STORYTELLING OR ENCOURAGE USER INVOLVEMENT?
NIKE'S "DREAM CRAZY"	BOLD STANCE ON SOCIAL JUSTICE, ALIGNING WITH TARGET AUDIENCE VALUES	HOW CAN YOU USE STORYTELLING OR ENCOURAGE USER INVOLVEMENT?
COCA-COLA'S "SHARE A COKE"	PERSONALIZATION, EMOTIONAL CONNECTION, SOCIAL MEDIA ENGAGEMENT	HOW CAN YOU PERSONALIZE YOUR CONTENT TO BUILD STRONGER CONNECTIONS WITH YOUR AUDIENCE?

STEP 2: ANALYZE CAMPAIGN PITFALLS

CAMPAIGN EXAMPLE	WHAT WENT WRONG?	WHAT CAN YOU LEARN FROM THIS?
PEPSI'S "LIVE FOR NOW"	TRIVIALIZED ACTIVISM, LACKED AUTHENTICITY	DON'T EXPLOIT SERIOUS ISSUES FOR COMMERCIAL GAIN. AUTHENTICITY IS KEY.
MCDONALD'S #MCDSTORIES	NEGATIVE USER-GENERATED CONTENT, NO CONTROL OVER MESSAGE	ALWAYS HAVE A MODERATION PLAN WHEN USING HASHTAGS OR USER CONTENT.
AMAZON'S FIRE PHONE	PRODUCT FAILURE, UNCLEAR VALUE PROPOSITION	ENSURE YOUR PRODUCT MEETS CUSTOMER NEEDS AND IS CLEARLY COMMUNICATED.
GAP'S LOGO REDESIGN	SUDDEN, UNTHOUGHT-OUT CHANGE TO A CLASSIC BRAND IMAGE	UNDERSTAND THE EMOTIONAL CONNECTION PEOPLE HAVE WITH YOUR BRAND BEFORE MAKING DRASTIC CHANGES.

STEP 3: NEXT STEPS

NOW THAT YOU'VE LEARNED FROM OTHERS, LIST ONE EXPERIMENT YOU'D LIKE TO TRY BASED ON WHAT YOU'VE LEARNED. IT COULD BE A CONTENT FORMAT, A NEW APPROACH, OR TESTING A BOLD MESSAGE.

8

THE 'HYPE' & THE 'HERE TO STAY'

FROM NOISE TO SIGNAL

CHAPTER VIII.
THE 'HYPE' & THE 'HERE TO STAY'

STAY AHEAD OF THE CURVE WITH EMERGING TECHNOLOGIES AND TRENDS

PREDICTIONS FOR THE FUTURE OF CONTENT MARKETING

As a small business owner, staying ahead of the curve with emerging technologies and trends is crucial to remaining relevant in an ever-changing digital landscape. But in a world full of flashy new technologies, how do you distinguish between what is just hype and what is truly worth your time? With so many new tools emerging every day, it's easy to get caught up in the excitement. However, understanding the difference between fleeting trends and technologies that will have a lasting impact can make or break your strategy.

One of the best ways to navigate this is by asking yourself: How will this help me be more efficient, more creative, or more effective in delivering value to my audience? That's where technologies like Artificial Intelligence (AI) come in. Unlike some of the technologies that may fizzle out in a year or two, AI is not just a passing trend—it's a powerful tool that's already reshaping how businesses operate, and it's here to stay.

When your resources are limited, AI acts as a reliable right hand, allowing you to do more with less. It automates tasks that would otherwise be time-consuming, such as content creation, data analysis, and customer segmentation. By taking on these repetitive tasks, AI frees you up to focus on the bigger picture—strategizing, engaging with customers, and crafting content that speaks to their needs. In other words, it's an extension of your team that works 24/7, ensuring that no opportunity goes unnoticed.

Even when your resources are plentiful, AI offers the gift of efficiency. It doesn't just help you get things done faster; it allows you to focus your energy where it matters most. For instance, AI can analyze large data sets to uncover trends and insights, enabling you to make informed decisions quickly. It can help you craft personalized experiences at scale, delivering content that resonates with your audience's unique preferences. The result? You get more meaningful interactions, increased engagement, and a stronger connection with your customers. By embracing AI, you're investing in a long-term solution that will not only improve your bottom line but will also create a sustainable competitive advantage.

EMERGING TECHNOLOGIES SHAPING CONTENT CREATION AND DISTRIBUTION

The digital landscape is evolving rapidly, and with it, so too are the ways we create and distribute content. Technologies like virtual reality (VR), augmented reality (AR), and AI are all playing a role in shaping the future of content marketing. But not all new technologies are created equal, and some may not be ready for widespread adoption just yet. It's important to weigh the potential benefits against the challenges of implementation.

Take VR and AR, for example. These technologies are groundbreaking and can provide immersive experiences that engage your audience in innovative ways. However, they require significant investment in terms of both time and money, and their impact may not be felt immediately. While VR and AR hold exciting potential, they may not yet be the right fit for every brand or industry, especially small businesses with limited budgets. Instead, focus on technologies that provide immediate, measurable results, such as AI and machine learning.

AI-powered content generation tools, for instance, have become indispensable for businesses looking to create high-quality content quickly and at scale. Whether you're generating blog posts, social media updates, or email newsletters, AI can assist in producing content that aligns with your brand voice and resonates with your audience. The days of spending hours brainstorming or writing content from scratch are over. With AI, you can generate ideas, write drafts, and even optimize content for SEO, all in a fraction of the time it would take manually.

Beyond content creation, AI can also transform how you distribute and promote your content. Through data analytics and predictive algorithms, AI can identify the best channels and times to distribute your content, ensuring it reaches the right audience. For example, AI can analyze your audience's past behavior to recommend the most relevant content, or it can predict when your audience is most likely to engage with your posts. This level of personalization and optimization would be difficult, if not impossible, to achieve without the power of AI.

HYPE AND LONG-TERM VALUE

With so many emerging technologies vying for attention, it's important to be discerning about where you invest your time and resources. This is where understanding the difference between "hype" and "here to stay" becomes crucial. Not every new technology or trend will live up to the promises of marketers or industry leaders. While it can be tempting to jump on the latest bandwagon, focusing on long-term, sustainable solutions is a more effective approach.

AI, for instance, isn't just a fad—it's fundamentally changing the way businesses operate. From automating mundane tasks to providing real-time insights into customer behavior, AI is transforming every facet of content marketing. The key is to embrace AI as a tool that amplifies your existing strengths. Rather than trying to implement every new trend that comes your way, focus on integrating technologies like AI that can help you streamline operations, deliver personalized content, and stay ahead of the competition.

Similarly, keep an eye on personalization. Consumers today demand tailored experiences, and businesses that can deliver personalized content are more likely to foster loyalty and engagement. But don't confuse personalization with gimmicky tactics—true personalization is data-driven, built on a foundation of trust and relevance. Technologies like AI and machine learning can help you deliver the right message to the right person at the right time, but it's essential to use these tools thoughtfully and ethically.

STRATEGIES FOR STAYING AHEAD

To stay ahead in a world of rapidly changing technologies, small business owners must cultivate a mindset of continuous learning, experimentation, and adaptation. It's not enough to simply know about the latest trends; you must understand how to apply them in ways that add value to your business and resonate with your audience.

START BY STAYING INFORMED

Subscribe to industry blogs, attend webinars and conferences, and engage with thought leaders and peers. The more knowledge you gain, the better equipped you'll be to make informed decisions about which technologies are worth exploring and which are just noise. Also, make time for experimentation. As a smaller operation, you have the advantage of being nimble and flexible. You can test new ideas, adapt quickly based on feedback, and refine your approach without the layers of bureaucracy that larger corporations face.

FOSTER A CULTURE OF INNOVATION

Encourage your team to think outside the box and embrace a "Why not?" mentality. When you create an environment that values experimentation and creativity, you'll unlock new possibilities and discover innovative ways to engage your audience. And don't be afraid to fail fast. Not every experiment will be a success, but each failure is an opportunity to learn and grow.

Finally, remember that the key to staying ahead isn't about jumping on every new trend—it's about choosing the right trends, integrating them strategically, and using them to create lasting value for your customers. By focusing on long-term, sustainable technologies like AI, personalization, and data analytics, you'll ensure that your business is positioned for success in the years to come.

REFLECTION: LOOKING TO THE FUTURE

As we venture into the future of content marketing, it's clear that emerging technologies like AI and data analytics are here to stay—and they're reshaping the landscape in ways we never imagined. But with so many trends vying for attention, it's easy to get overwhelmed. The key is not to chase every shiny new tool but to focus on the technologies that can bring long-term value and efficiency to your business.

Remember, the future isn't about perfection; it's about progress. Stay curious, keep learning, and experiment with strategies that align with your goals. It's through thoughtful adaptation and the smart use of emerging technologies that you'll continue to stay ahead of the curve. So, what's next? Keep evolving your approach, embrace new tools like AI to streamline your efforts, and most importantly, keep delivering value to your audience. After all, that's what it's all about.

ACTION STEP:

WRITE DOWN ONE EMERGING TECHNOLOGY OR TREND YOU'RE EXCITED ABOUT (E.G., AI PERSONALIZATION). THEN, LIST **THREE WAYS** IT COULD IMPROVE YOUR CONTENT STRATEGY. FINALLY, PLAN ONE SMALL EXPERIMENT TO TEST IT OVER THE NEXT THREE MONTHS.

CONCLUSION

TO SUM IT UP

As we come to the conclusion of From Noise to Signal, let's take a moment to recap the key points covered in this book. We began by emphasizing the importance of understanding your audience, delving into their world, pinpointing their pain points and desires, and creating detailed buyer personas. We then explored the essentials of crafting compelling messages, including defining your brand voice and tone, developing a unique selling proposition (USP), and leveraging storytelling techniques to engage your audience.

Throughout this journey, we've emphasized the significance of creating high-impact content that resonates deeply with your audience. In a crowded digital landscape, capturing attention is more challenging than ever, but it's also more rewarding. By prioritizing authenticity, creativity, and strategic thinking, you can cut through the noise and forge meaningful connections with your audience that drive business results and feed the bottom line.

I encourage you to take action on the strategies and insights discussed within its pages. Whether you're a seasoned marketer or a small business owner just starting out, there's always room to refine and improve your content marketing efforts.

Do the exercises and take the time to conduct audience research, define your brand voice, and experiment with new technologies and tactics. Remember, success doesn't happen overnight, but with dedication, perseverance, and a willingness to learn, you can create content that not only catches your customer's attention but also leaves a lasting positive reputation and impact that helps you retain them for years to come.

Thank you for taking this journey with me. And here's to your continued success in creating high-impact content that takes your customer engagement to the next level!

REFERENCES

Austen, I. (2014, July 10). Coca-Cola's "Share a Coke" campaign hits new heights in personal ization. The New York Times. https://www.nytimes.com/2014/07/10/business/coca-colas-share-a-coke-campaign-hits-new-heights-in-personalization.html

Bertolucci, J. (2012, January 25). McDonald's #McDStories Twitter campaign: A lesson in social media disaster. Social Media Today. https://www.socialmediatoday.com/content/mc donalds-mcdstories-twitter-campaign-lesson-social-media-disaster

Cohen, R. (2019, September 1). LEGO celebrates creativity with "Rebuild the World" campaign. Adweek. https://www.adweek.com/brand-marketing/lego-celebrates-creativi ty-with-rebuild-the-world-campaign/

Hawkins, A. J. (2012, October 14). Red Bull Stratos space jump: How the stunt captivated mil lions. The Verge. https://www.theverge.com/2012/10/14/3497760/red-bull-stratos-space-jump-event-video

HuffPost. (2017, April 5). Pepsi pulls controversial ad with Kendall Jenner after backlash. Huff Post. https://www.huffpost.com/entry/pepsi-pulls-kendall-jen ner-ad_n_58e79e16e4b0e0d4cdadab7d

Leung, R. (2016, October 5). Airbnb's Live There campaign: The emotional and experiential appeal of travel. Medium. https://medium.com/airbnb-employee-blog/airbnbs-live-there-campaign-the-emotional-and-experiential-appeal-of-travel-4fb4e173c8b7

Smith, D. (2015, March 4). Burger King's "Subservient Chicken" and the lessons in viral mar keting. Business Insider. https://www.businessinsider.com/burger-kings-subservi ent-chicken-and-the-lessons-in-viral-marketing-2015-3

Sweeney, L. (2014, July 23). Amazon's Fire Phone: A $200 million flop. TechCrunch. https://techcrunch.com/2014/07/23/amazons-fire-phone-a-200-million-flop/

Zengler, T. (2010, October 12). Why Gap's logo redesign failed so spectacularly. Fast Company. https://www.fastcompany.com/1706441/why-gaps-logo-redesign-failed-so-spectacu larly

DIGITAL CONTENT

SCAN THIS QR CODE TO GET EXCLUSIVE ACCESS TO THE ELECTRONIC VERSION OF THE WORKSHEETS IN THIS BOOK.

CONVENIENTLY DOWNLOAD, PRINT, AND FILL OUT THE EXERCISES DIGITALLY, OR SAVE THEM TO YOUR DEVICE FOR EASY REFERENCE ANYTIME.

ENHANCE YOUR LEARNING EXPERIENCE WITH THIS INTERACTIVE TOOL AND TAKE YOUR CONTENT STRATEGY TO THE NEXT LEVEL!

www.ingramcontent.com/pod-product-compliance
Lightning Source LLC
Chambersburg PA
CBHW072000220326
41599CB00034BA/7069

* 9 7 9 8 2 1 8 6 7 5 4 6 2 *